Presenting the Catholic Faith
A Modern Catechism for Inquirers

Frank P. DeSiano, C.S.P.

Paulist Press ◊ New York ◊ Mahwah

NIHIL OBSTAT
Francis J. McAree, S.T.D.

IMPRIMATUR
† Joseph T. O'Keefe, D.D.
Vicar General, Archdiocese of New York

September 11, 1986

The Nihil Obstat and Imprimatur are official declarations that a book or pamphlet is free of doctrinal or moral error. No implication is contained therein that those who have granted the Nihil Obstat and Imprimatur agree with the contents, opinions or statements expressed.

Library of Congress
Catalog Card Number 86-62554

ISBN: 0-8091-2841-1

Published by Paulist Press
997 Macarthur Boulevard
Mahwah, New Jersey 07430

Printed and bound in the
United States of America

I DEDICATE THIS SMALL BOOK
TO THE PEOPLE OF
SAINT PAUL THE APOSTLE PARISH
IN NEW YORK CITY
WHERE THE PAULIST COMMUNITY BEGAN
AND WHERE THE PAULIST VISION
IS CONSTANTLY RENEWED
THROUGH THE LIFE AND INQUIRY
OF ITS PARISHIONERS

Contents

Acknowledgements

Biblical citations have come, generally, from *The New American Bible* (1970, Confraternity of Christian Doctrine) which is most widely used in Catholic worship. Some words in the text have been altered, according to the meaning of the original biblical language, to provide clarity or emphasis. Citations from Catholic rituals all follow the translation of the International Committee on English in the Liturgy.

In addition to invaluable suggestions received from the editors of the Paulist Press, I have also been greatly aided by Ida Cerone who, against all odds, worked to make my grammar and word usage clearer than it usually is. Try as she did to catch all errors and lapses, alas, I fear I have snuck some by her anyhow.

Introduction

This little book is intended to accomplish a very specific goal. As it claims, it seeks to *present the Catholic faith*.

I want this book to do a very modest task: to *help the person who wants to be introduced to the Catholic faith*, to help the person who is inquiring.

I have long felt that there is no book readily available for someone in this situation, that most books want to cover everything or that they are not presenting things from the point of view of the inquirer.

Some books that seem to be for "inquirers" actually are not for them. They were written as teaching tools, and they contain many issues and questions that, frankly, inquirers who are seeking initial information just do not want.

Some books, too, are written in such a way that all the dogmas of the Church are covered, not in such a way that the faith is *presented*. Rather, it is "covered."

Some books are straight catechisms (question-and-answer books) and it seems easy to lose the woods for all the trees that are presented in that format. At the same time, the question-and-answer format, used expeditiously, is a fine way to help a person get acquainted with the faith at his or her own pace.

I am, in the book, concerned with the *inquirer*—the person who is open enough to ask questions, to seek information, to want to know more about Catholics and their Church.

That is why I subtitle this book "A Modern Catechism for Inquirers"; in rather plain language, in a straightforward way, with the need of the inquirer in mind, the Catholic faith is presented. If there is a special place in heaven for those who want to write simply and directly, I hope to gain it.

This is an "ice-breaker" book: to help people get introduced to the Catholic faith, as much as possible, on their terms. Aside from trying to use plain language, I have also tried to pose the questions as I have actually heard people ask them. Rather than letting the doctrine control the questions, I want the questions to shape the presentation of the doctrine.

I am presuming that an "inquirer" has an open mind and also has the resources to go on further. Other people to talk with. Other books to get into. Other programs to join that will continue this search.

Because this book wants to be only the "starting answer" (and not the "final" one, if there ever could be a final answer) it directs an inquirer further, where he or she can grow as God calls in the future.

I suggest for now two big helps. One, get a Bible—a modern, readable translation that you can refer to as you read this book and talk to others. Two, drop in on Catholic worship on Sunday or even on a weekday. Attend Mass and try to observe what is happening—and *share* what is happening. If it helps, you can use the outline of the Mass in this book.

Recently, the Catholic Church joined other modern organizations in creating a kind of "alphabet-soup" vocabulary the way the New Deal gave us the CCC and WPO and the FDIC. Along with other alphabetical offerings, the Church now has something called RCIA—the Rite of Christian Initiation of Adults. This is a program for preparing to join the Church, especially directed at the non-baptized.

In this program, one not only deals with questions in detail, one also prays, reflects, serves and grows spiritually with a group of believers. This program actually brings about initiation into the Church through the process of spiritual growth.

This little book belongs at the very start of such a program, if an inquirer should seek to begin the RCIA. It belongs at the appetizer level, what one uses to get ready for a banquet of insight, study and growth.

It also belongs in the hands of others who are "inquiring" in their own ways—perhaps they are already Catholics but they haven't been truly formed in that rich tradition, or perhaps they were even waylaid in their Catholic growth.

Inquirers need time, need to pace themselves, need to absorb and question at their own rate, and need to have trust in a God who trusts them in their search.

Which brings us back to the idea of an inquirer: a seeker, one who quests after the true and the real. And one with an open mind. No one knows where the inquiry will lead—yet that is the exciting part of inquiring. But the inquiry will make sense only to the extent that inquirers respect their own search, the questions of their minds and the longings of their hearts.

I have tried to respect mind and heart in this book: God knows enough games are played with people's souls these days. I trust, too, that the reader will respect the search of mind and heart and, after the ice has been broken, will find a way to truth, happiness and peace of spirit.

1

The Community of the Church

(*Scripture Reading:*
In the Book of Acts, Chapter 2, the
Holy Spirit gathers people from all
nations around the early
community of Jesus.)

W e each drive or walk by churches every day. We imagine that we know what a church is. We see them all the time. They are brick or stone, steepled or flat.

Ask anyone about a church and you will get some remark about a building where there is an altar or a pulpit and people go there on Sunday mornings.

In most of our minds, then, a church is a building, and a particular kind of building—one that looks different and one that is for a certain kind of people.

The Church Is a Community

A church needs buildings for much of its work. It is not, however, a building. The *building* of a church means nothing without the *community* of a church.

A community is nothing else than a group of people who belong to each other. People who have needs, feelings, beliefs, hopes and pains. People who have connections with each other. When our church buildings lose their communities, they become museum-like buildings—pretty to look at, but not places in which to feel at home.

Church communities have existed for a long time. In all of history, we see groups of people who gathered together because

5

of what they believed. Sometimes these communities were very large, but they all came down to the very real contacts between very real people.

The Christian Church is a community that has existed since the time of Jesus. We see him gathering followers and friends who felt they belonged with him. He made them feel welcomed. He made them feel part of himself. He made them feel that their deepest questions were being answered. (For example, Matthew 9:9–13; John 21:8–11)

After his death and resurrection, his followers continued as his community. They met together to pray, to remember the words and deeds of Jesus. They sang hymns and they worshiped. They formed groups in which each Christian had a place as if a member of the family. (See Acts 2:42–47) Most important, they felt that they continued to have contact with Jesus, that he made them one family by their sharing in his Holy Spirit.

Community for Everyone

One of the first questions faced by the followers of Jesus was: Who could belong to the family of Jesus? Who were members of his community?

Some people felt that, like Jesus and his first followers, you had to be Jewish to belong to his family. Once you became a Jew, you could understand the message of Jesus.

Important as it is to understand Jesus' Jewish roots, others still maintained that Jesus, after he rose from the dead, became the Lord of all. Because of that, a person only needed to have a true relationship with Jesus in order to be a member of his family. In fact, people without any Jewish faith were coming to believe in Jesus and receiving the Holy Spirit that he sent. (Acts 15:3–12)

This made it all the more clear that, with Jesus, something new had happened in religion. It was not going to be based on race or nationality; it was going to be freed from culture and from custom.

The Church of Jesus, in other words, would be for everyone. Whatever the race, whatever the age, whatever the social position, whatever the background, whatever the language, this faith would belong to anyone who would accept it. It would belong to anyone who accepted a true relationship with Jesus.

Of course there were churches in different cities—we remember their ancient names like Antioch, Ephesus, Corinth, Alexandria and Rome. (The community in Jerusalem was scattered just as was the whole population of Jerusalem after it was attacked and destroyed in 70 A.D.) But all the members of the Christian community knew they belonged to the same Church.

If you open a Bible to the New Testament, you will see a group of writings that list some of the people of these ancient Christian communities—Romans, Galatians, Corinthians, etc. All these letters were written by St. Paul who labored to set up all these communities. St. Paul preached the same message wherever he went and his care for the churches he founded shows that they were very much tied together.

The word "catholic" tries to say what the Christian community is like: a community for everyone. A community of all peoples, in all nations, of all ages, through all cultures. So great, then, is the impact of the resurrection of Jesus that it can touch every person. So great is the impact of the risen Jesus that *he* can touch all people and invite them into his own community, the Church.

Was it only coincidence that this community of Jesus began at the time of Roman power? Was it only coincidence that the Roman Empire had already begun to link up many different peoples? Surely, the impact of the vast and unifying Roman Empire helped the early Christians to see that their own communities were linked. Maybe it took two months to go from one Christian community to another—but when you got there, you belonged!

The early Christian faith spread with great leaps in those early centuries. It went around the whole ancient Roman world and entered into all those different cultures. It also developed channels of communication and direction so that, in spite of many disagreements and differences, the Christians could stay as one; could stay, that is, as the *one family* that God called them to be. If there is, after all, only one Jesus, why should there be many different families that claim him as their one and only Lord? (See Ephesians 4:5–6)

If this Church was a community for everybody, how could groups start cutting off other groups?

Catholic and Christian

The unity that was part of the early community of Jesus was naturally tested. Families have spats; Christian families have had spats—and outright fights. In spite of this, Catholics see themselves as part of the unbroken tradition of the family life of the Christian Church. They see themselves back in Rome and Antioch and Alexandria.

They also see themselves through all the centuries, in ancient Greece and Syria, at the time of Rome's fall, through the Dark Ages and the brilliant Middle Ages, in the Renaissance and Reformation, in the Enlightenment and the waves of emigrants to the Americas, in the expanding continents of Africa and Asia and, with spunk, in whatever brave New World is to come.

The Catholic family is old, but also new. It is classical and modern as well. It contains the most elegant and the most simple, the most educated and the least. The Catholic family has touched upon every culture on every shore, leaving something of itself and picking so much up.

Strangely, some people don't think of Catholics as Christians. Too much ritual, too many strange ceremonies, too clear a doctrine—or too loose! But the family history is all there, the history of a community of people who have persistently followed Jesus and found themselves belonging to him—and to each other. This little book may help shed understanding on the rituals and doctrines, beliefs and practices which are, perhaps, not any stranger than what any other community evolves during a life as long as two thousand years.

Maybe, too, by "inquiring" into the Catholic Christian community, some of the unity lost in its history might be retrieved. For high on the agenda of all the Christian family, Catholic and not, is the goal of living the faith so truly and so clearly that all the members of the family might see how they are related and come back together again. With any sincere inquiry, the traits of the family start to show!

Questions

What does "catholic" mean?

"Catholic" comes from ancient Greek words ("kath" and "holon") that mean "for all the people." A church which uses the name "catholic" must be open to all people.

What is the Catholic Church?

The Catholic Church is composed of those who come from the most ancient Christian lineage, tracing their faith to the first followers of Jesus, the apostles, and the earliest communities of the apostles. Their community life, expressed in their worship, their teaching and Church organization, reflects this ancient heritage and the continuity of their life from apostolic times.

What is the Roman Catholic Church?

The Roman Catholic Church is the Christian community that traces its roots to the apostolic community in Rome and the apostles of Rome, St. Peter and St. Paul. The unity all Catholics have with the Pope, the bishop of Rome, shows these roots.

Are Catholics Christians?

Catholics are Christians. They base their whole faith and way of life on Jesus Christ.

What do Catholics have in common with other Christians?

Catholics share with their brothers and sisters in the Orthodox traditions an ancient heritage, a tradition of sacred rites (called *sacraments*), a devotion to holy men and women of the faith, and a deep sense of the sacred. With their Protestant brothers and sisters, Catholics share, among other things, a deep reverence for the Holy Bible, a belief in God's constant care and gracious love, a respect for individual conscience and a strong concern for the welfare of others.

THE ECUMENICAL MOVEMENT

Christianity has suffered from divisions since its beginning. These divisions solidified, first in 1054 A.D. when the Eastern and Western churches fell into disunion (the Eastern churches are called "orthodox"); then, in the sixteenth century, when the great Protestant* Reformation began numerous separations within the Western church itself.

In the early twentieth century, however, the Protestant churches began a process of reuniting in the "Faith and Order" movement. This process continues, bearing fruit through (1) greater cooperation and potential unity among several of the main Protestant churches and (2) the increasing involvement of the Roman Catholic and Orthodox churches in this ecumenical movement in recent decades.

Today the Roman Catholic Church is in dialogue with all the major Protestant churches and also with non-Christian religions such as Judaism and Islam; it has affirmed the Orthodox (Eastern) churches as "sister" churches.

Most Christian churches are pursuing unity seriously because disunity is such a scandal.

*"*Protestant*" refers to that movement of churches against certain abuses and teachings of the Roman Catholic Church in the sixteenth century.

How do you characterize Catholics?

Catholics come from all levels of society and are all over the world. They have a strong sense of being a religious family; their faith is expressed through their personal and communal lives. Catholics think of *time* in very broad terms, focusing on both ancient traditions and modern problems. While aware of their history, they also worry about the future of the world. Catholics have a natural feeling for the *sacred,* and they believe God is very present in the world. Catholics also emphasize *a deep spiritual tradition,* believing that everyone is called to holiness and that God's Spirit is present in the life of every believer. They express their faith in the unity they have with each other, with their bishops and with the Bishop of Rome. Catholics do not consider themselves simply a gathering of individuals; they are first members of the Church, the community of Jesus.

Whom do Catholics think can be saved?

Catholics think everyone can be saved if he or she strives to know God and is faithful to the relationship God has with that person. God wants to save everyone.

Does God save those who are not Catholics?

God saves all who respond to his love.

How does it help to be Catholic?

From the faith, Scriptures, traditions and support that Catholics find in their Church, they know God's love in a *clear way*—and they are helped to respond to that love deeply and consistently. The sacraments they share and the guidance of their ministers also ratify the love and strength they receive from God. Without supports like these, it is difficult to keep God's love clearly before us and it is even more difficult to respond to that love faithfully. Because of the role the Church plays in our salvation, Catholics see the Church as an essential way of truly finding God and living his love.

What does it mean "to be *saved*"?

Most basically, "being saved" means being free from a threatening or distressing situation—for example, pain, persecution, illness or the prospect of death. In addition, Catholics mean that they have been freed from the most stressful and difficult problems of life: sin, oppression, ignorance and death. While we do not experience the fullness of "being saved" in this life, Catholics believe that salvation begins now and will find its sure fulfillment in heaven.

What is needed to enter the Catholic Church?

Only faith is needed to enter the Catholic Church. Because of *their* faith, parents can seek the entrance of their children into the Church.

Jesus is described in the Gospel of Luke in the words of Simeon which show his impact on all people:

" . . . *a revealing light to the Gentiles and the glory of your people Israel.*"

(Luke 2:30–32)

St. Paul also writes:

" . . . *for God wants all people to be saved and to come to know the truth . . .*"

(1 Timothy 2:4)

"*The grace of God has appeared, offering salvation to all people. . . . It was Jesus who sacrificed himself for us, to redeem us all from all unrighteousness and to cleanse for himself a people of his own, eager to do what is right.*"

(Titus 2:11, 14)

2

Faith

(*Scripture Reading:*
The Book of Exodus, Chapter 3,
tells of Moses' encounter with à
God who reveals himself in caring
for the oppressed Hebrews.)

M ost people are believers. They believe almost everything in their lives. In fact, they need faith in order to live.

Let's say that knowledge is what we have found out through our own observation and conclusions. Well, no matter how many years we have lived, we have not had enough time to investigate anything more than a fraction of reality. We have only the perceptions that we have had, the energy that we have put into organizing these perceptions, and the sharpness with which we have insights and come to conclusions from these same perceptions.

If we never, for example, went to Miami, how do we know there *is* a Miami! Obviously, *people* have told us. That's precisely the way we find out most of what we know: people tell us.

Now what we know through ourselves we call plain and simple knowledge. What we know through the experiences of others, we call knowledge as well, but it is based on a kind of faith.

What if we had to, for example, start at ground zero with everything that everyone has discovered. Go back before two sticks were rubbed together, before the proverbial wheel was invented, before languages were developed, before any scientific knowledge was developed, before any history was told. What would we know? Very little!

Even more, if the human race had constantly to return to

13

ground zero in order to make sure its knowledge was based on its cold and hard observations, the human race would still be making doodles in caves—if that!

In this way, we can think of faith as a kind of communication between members of the human family. A way of swapping knowledge or insights. A way of knowing through others.

So when we get the bus in the morning or read the newspaper, when we visit a new city or get a letter from a friend, when we learn a new game or turn our computers on, we are engaged in this broad sense of faith.

Religious faith is not that much different. Surely, we can perhaps buy a ticket to Miami and *know* that it exists. But we cannot so easily verify, for example, whether there are angels. And yet, we verify very little of what we absorb in life and religion deals with a special kind of verification.

Religion is not just about "facts" such as when Jesus lived and the kind of cross he was nailed to. It is about the *meaning* of those facts—a meaning which touches upon the very basic questions of life. Who are we? Is there a purpose to our lives? Are we unique? What is our destiny? Are we loved? Are we worthy of love? If we are valuable, what does that mean for the way we act?

Questions such as these are more important, really, than whether there is a city called Miami to which we can travel. For questions such as these determine the way we will live, whether in Miami or Memphis or Madagascar! Questions such as these affect the very way we understand ourselves.

Now philosophy can play around with these questions, and the playings of philosophers give us sharper questions and a better vocabulary.

But no one can engage in all these questions and none of the answers can be "verified" by a simple plane trip. Yet it is possible that some of us who ask these questions can find answers—for we would not have these questions if we were not meant to somehow be dealing with them and searching for their answers.

How do answers come? Perhaps through enough diddling—or perhaps through our contact with a deeper Being who provides an approach to such answers.

After all, our minds are wide open and our hearts are ever expansive. Maybe we are antennas for deeper reality than what we can immediately see before our noses.

If people have religious breakthroughs, we call it revelation because it *does* come from beyond their own experiments and knowledge. Revelation comes from God and God's contact with us. It is his relationship with us and the effects of that relationship on who we are and what we "know."

Revelation could not happen without some kind of vocabulary. Indeed, without some kinds of names or words we have relatively little in our heads. Revelation needs the gradual shaping of human words and ideas, imagination and poetry, so that we will be open to the effects of God's relationship with us.

Christians believe that this kind of relationship happened between the Jewish people and their God and that the part of the Bible which they call the "Old Testament" represents the revelation, the words and concepts, that made such a relationship possible and also flowed from that relationship. (See Hebrews 1:1–3)

The relationship established by God with the Jews was the background for Jesus whom Christians understand as the fullest revelation of God. In Jesus, Christians believe that God spoke completely, becoming intimately one with the human family in his "Son," as Jesus is proclaimed to be.

Indeed, the very word "Son" wants to say that Jesus brings the very "godness" of God into our world.

So along with the Old Testament, the revelation of Jesus fulfills in a dramatic way the faith we have about God. The record of Jesus' life and words, as well as the experiences of his first followers, is in the part of the Bible we call the "New Testament."

The Bible, then, is not just an extremely fascinating book that Christians find exciting. The Bible, rather, forms the whole background of the believer's attitude toward life and God. The words of the believer come from the Bible. The words that shape the basic way a believer sees, thinks and acts all come from the Bible.

In fact, without the book of revelation which we call the Bible, the Christian could not be a believer. The Christian would be an entirely different species, not only with a God named and known differently, but with a heart and mind shaped differently.

The Bible, in this way, becomes the "founding document" of the Christian's faith. Like a constitution, the Bible's sacred words, opening up God's communication with us, form the ground on which a Christian stands.

In its words, images, experiences, ideas and forms there is unraveled a whole range of religious feeling that lies open to anyone who reads the Bible. Through its ideas, doctrines, approaches and traditions, the Bible continues to form the Christian family, reinforcing its contact with the events and interpretations of religious experience that alone make sense for a community of faith.

In its chapters and verses, we find Adam and Moses, Judith and Samson, David and Jezebel, Abraham and Daniel; in its stories and lessons we find a people called into a religious family through their divinely-led escape from Egypt, a people called back from the bleakest exile by divinely-given mercy, a people called to the future by a divinely-inspired hope that, one day, true fullness and freedom would come to us by salvation.

Such salvation rests, for members of the Christian family, in Jesus. The complete revelation of God to us is embodied in the flesh and blood of our own nature in the Christ.

The Christian's faith revolves about him, centers on him, dwells in his center: his heart, his vision, his words, his deeds, his life, his risen life. In Jesus, the Christian finds that the special kind of knowing-through-another is verified by the special kind of knowing-through-Jesus that means living-in-Jesus—which is what Christians mean by faith.

And in Jesus the Christian finds a sort of verification of faith. For the kinds of words and deeds that we have in Jesus, the kind of being he shows and brings us in himself, make for answers to those essential questions that burn beneath the human spirit. In his answers, the believer finds answers unable to be found anywhere else.

What is more, in the enterprise of faith, by which we come to know through the community of others, the Christian finds the family of Jesus, those who have received and shared his word from the very first gathering of those about him. In knowing through the testimony and faith of others, we come to know them, to belong to them, to be one with them. We are, thereby, joined not only with the Lord, but with all those also joined to him by faith and life.

Questions

What is faith?

Most simply, faith is putting trust in another, such as the trust that a child has in its mother, or the trust that we place in teachers or friends. For Christians, faith means the complete trust that we have in an absolutely loving God. Faith also implies *why* we have trust—the kinds of things we believe about God or Jesus that cause us to put our trust in him.

ON FAITH

The Letter to the Hebrews says:

> "Faith is confident assurance concerning what we hope for and conviction about things we do not see. Because of their faith, men of old were approved by God. Through faith, we perceive that the worlds were created by the word of God and that what is visible came into being through the invisible."
>
> (Hebrews 13:1–2)

Abraham is called the "father of faith" because his response to God's call entailed deep faith and trust. St. Paul comments about his faith:

> "Hoping against hope, Abraham believed and so became the father of many nations, just as it was once told him, 'Numerous as this shall your descendants be.' . . . He never questioned or doubted God's promise; rather, he was strengthened in faith and gave glory to God, fully persuaded that God could do whatever he had promised. Thus his faith was credited to him as justice."
>
> (Romans 4:18–22)

For the story of Abraham, see Genesis 12 and the following chapters in the opening book of the Bible.

To know God, for example, as a loving Father who personally cares for us helps us to know *why* we put our trust in him.

Is faith an unusual thing?

Faith is a very normal thing, a natural attitude of mind. Because we cannot verify everything in life, we need faith. We need to depend on the word and wisdom of those around us. We need to depend on—trust—others.

Why do people have faith in God?

Even with all degrees of wisdom and knowledge, people still cannot cope with or even express some problems, some insights or some discoveries because they are simply too deep. For this reason, people have had to look beyond themselves, beyond human life itself, to find the wisdom and strength to deal with these vast issues. In this way, humans have found themselves searching for full truth and meaning. Our human race and our world is open to receive the help and revelation that Christians attribute to a divine being, to God. This openness to God is the basis of faith.

Can we live without faith?

No. Our human experiences are just too limited and our lives are just too short for us to know everything for ourselves or rediscover what others have discovered and left for us. So everyone needs faith of one sort or another. Some people feel they can live without religious faith, without faith in some divine being. A Christian thinks, however, that everyone is in some way a believer. In one way or another, we all make assumptions about life that imply faith. For instance, we assume we will have a future, or that life makes sense, or that justice and goodness are important; these and other fundamental assumptions about life cannot be verified, yet they are behind all human thinking and living.

Why do some people find faith difficult?

Faith is a gift from God and not some theory we have invented. Believing is not completely in our control. If faith is

---

A STORY ABOUT FAITH

*"The other disciples kept telling Thomas: 'We have seen the Lord.'
Thomas answered, 'I will never believe it without probing the nail-
prints in his hands and without putting my finger into the nailmarks
and my hand into his side.' A week later, the disciples were once
more in the room, and this time Thomas was with them. Despite the
locked doors, Jesus came and stood before them. 'Peace be with you,'
he said. Then, to Thomas: 'Take your finger and examine my hands.
Put your hand into my side. Do not persist in your unbelief, but
believe!' Thomas said in response: 'My Lord and my God!' Jesus
said to him: 'You became a believer because you saw me. Blest are
they who have not seen and have believed.'"* (John 20:25–29)

---

difficult to find, still every person can search sincerely for
what seems true and good; sometimes that is all a person can
attain. Sometimes it happens that a person has experiences
that make faith difficult, such as parents who were not believers or a negative experience with religion.

Can people be made to believe?

No one can make another person believe. Because faith
is such a deeply personal act of trust, it must be done freely.
To force someone to believe is to twist the very idea of
faith.

Do children have faith?

Children come to faith by the example and faith of their parents. Parents provide their children with many good (and
some not-so-good) things before they are old enough to
choose for themselves; in the same way, parents can guide
their children in faith. Once children have begun to mature,
however, they must make their own act of faith.

WORDS OF FAITH

How do you find out what Catholics believe?

The core of the Catholic faith can be found in the ancient creeds which come from the Bible. To know all that Catholics believe, however, would take a lifetime of reflection on the Bible and the living tradition of the Catholic family.

What is a creed?

A creed is a short statement of faith used by a believing community to show the unity of their faith. All believers, for example, in that community would accept the same creed. Even in the New Testament, the beginnings of creeds are found, such as the formula, "Jesus is Lord." (For example, Philippians 2:11 and Romans 10:9) Catholics have used

---

CREEDS

Catholics regularly use two creeds, the Apostles' Creed and the "Nicean" Creed. The "Nicean" Creed (recited at Sunday worship) actually is the formula of faith affirmed by the bishops at their meeting in Constantinople in 381 A.D. It expands the shorter Creed which we popularly call the Apostles' Creed:

I believe in God, the Father Almighty, Creator of heaven and earth.
And in Jesus Christ, his only Son, our Lord, who was born of the Virgin Mary, suffered under Pontius Pilate, was crucified, died and was buried.
He descended into hell.
On the third day, he rose again from the dead.
He ascended into heaven and is seated at the right hand of the Father from where he will come to judge the living and the dead.
I believe in the Holy Spirit, the holy, catholic Church, the communion of saints, the forgiveness of sins, the resurrection of the body, and life everlasting.
Amen.

many creeds that come from the ancient Church; these creeds summarize certain important Christian beliefs. Many things believed by Christians are *not* in these creeds.

Do Catholics believe in the Bible?

Catholics do indeed believe in the Bible. Catholics understand that God was present in the experience of the Jewish people, guiding their history and their leaders, so that they could comprehend the special relationship he had with them—and wanted to have with all people. These leaders and writers, inspired by God, interpreted his mighty and loving acts in their history—how he freed them from slavery in Egypt, led them into a special land, dwelt in their sacred temple, and promised salvation even when they suffered defeat. These accounts are a "faith history" of the Israelite people. Remembering and retelling this faith history, the leaders and writers of the Jewish people preserved and reflected on these accounts. They were inspired by God to produce the very rich book we call the Old Testament or the Hebrew Scriptures, the story of the Jewish people up to the time of Jesus. The story of Jesus and the experiences of his followers is told in that part of the Bible we call the New Testament. This collection of writings, too, was done under the inspiration of God.

What is revelation?

Revelation is the action of God upon a particular people or person by which he communicates who he is.

Do you have to read the Bible to be saved?

No. Salvation is not something that you "earn" by any action, even by reading the Bible. Salvation comes from the grace of God. Millions of people do not know how to read, yet God will, in his wisdom and grace, bring them to salvation.

Do Catholics take the Bible literally?

Catholics take the Bible as it was meant to be taken. The Bible was composed under God's inspiration by the Jewish and first Christian people; this happened over many years and was guided by the experience of their respective communities. In the process, many kinds of writing, called "literary forms," were used (such as poetry, short story, legend, family tree, song, history). Understanding the Bible means understanding what the inspired author intended. This is the true "literal" meaning of the Bible. Basically, the Bible exists to teach us *religious* truth.

What is the value of the Bible?

The Bible, as God's revelation in the words of people who have experienced this revelation, opens the human spirit to the deepest dimensions of meaning and purpose. Through the Bible we come to know not only how others related to God, but how we can relate to him in our own lives. The teachings revealed by the Bible expand the possibilities of our own lives with others and with God. Without the Bible, it is scarcely possible to know God as he has revealed himself.

What is inspiration?

Inspiration is the process by which God caused the Sacred Scriptures of the Bible to be written, using the experiences, vocabulary and culture of the Jewish and early Christian people.

What language was the Bible written in?

The Bible was written in three languages: Hebrew and Aramaic (in the Old Testament), and Greek (in the New Testament).

Did God only choose the Jewish people?

God revealed himself in a special way to the Jewish people, but he was choosing *all people* when he chose them. The Scriptures frequently mention this. In mysterious ways, God

ABOUT THE BIBLE

The word "Bible" means "the books"—and this is literally the case, since the Bible is composed of many shorter works collected together. These works were produced at different times; sometimes even one of the books of the Bible was itself written in parts at different times and then collected into a single book.

If you open a Bible to its table of contents, you will see that it is divided into two parts, the *Old Testament,* which talks about God's relations with the Jewish people before the coming of Jesus, and the *New Testament,* which talks about Jesus and his early followers.

There are two traditions behind the Old Testament, the Hebrew tradition which contains thirty-nine books; and the Greek tradition, which contains forty-six books. Neither tradition was completely formed and settled at the time of Jesus. He refers to books in the Hebrew and the Greek tradition, as well as other books that are now part of neither tradition. Catholics and Orthodox follow the Greek tradition of the Old Testament.

The followers of Jesus and the first Christians finished the New Testament in Greek, relying heavily on the Greek tradition of the Bible which, while containing all the books in the Hebrew tradition, also contains the seven other books of the Greek tradition which were popular and accepted as holy in early Christian times.

The New Testament is similarly a collection of shorter works, twenty-seven in all.

The *Old Testament* consists of:

◇ The Torah, or Pentateuch, which contains the first five and most important books of the Old Testament. They touch on God's creation, the time of the Jewish forefathers, the escape of the Jews from Egypt and the covenant (pact) between God and them at Mount Sinai.
◇ The Histories, which talk about the conquest of the Holy Land and the days of the kings and thereafter.
◇ The Prophets, which contain words of those sent to correct Israel and call it back to its true faith.
◇ The Writings, which span a great amount of time and contain sacred hymns (called "psalms"), advice on daily life and books exploring deep religious questions.

The *New Testament* contains:

◊ The Gospels, which are the books about Jesus' ministry, death and resurrection, written by Matthew, Mark, Luke and John.
◊ The Letters, which were written by leaders of the early Church to newly founded communities to guide them in faith (most notably, St. Paul).
◊ One "history" book, The Acts of the Apostles, which follows St. Luke's Gospel and was written by him to present the formation and missionary activities of the early Church.
◊ One "prophetic" book, called Revelation, which interprets the events of ancient times in view of God's plan and care so as to encourage persecuted believers.

There are many new and fine translations of the Bible. We should read the one that speaks most clearly to us.

was also present in the history of other peoples, even though they did not come to know it and describe it as the Jewish people did. In an equally mysterious way, God is present in the life of everyone, even though a person may not explicitly know God or find words to express him.

3

Jesus

(*Scripture Reading:* The Sermon on the Mount, in Matthew's Gospel, Chapters 5, 6, and 7, are the best introduction to the mind of Jesus.)

E ven those of us without a shred of religious faith would have little difficulty calling Jesus a "nice guy."

Our imaginings of him (that is all they are) paint him as gentle, clean, clear of conviction, handsome, inspiring, and even blue-eyed and blond.

He doesn't go around hurting people (first qualification for being a "nice guy"); he rarely loses his temper (when he does, we are kind enough to say that it is "justified"), he never steals or lies, he never sullies his reputation.

He seems to have been *liked* by almost everyone. Even his would-be enemies were impressed with him. When they would come out to "test" him or "trip him up," he would manage such a fine answer, such a clever rejoinder, that they gave up their attack and, sometimes, left in absolute amazement. (See Mark 12:28–34)

All "nice guys" are popular. Jesus, when he began his public ministry, was immensely popular. People traveled all the way from southern Judea up to northern Galilee just to hear him, just to see him do wonders, just to have him touch them. (See Matthew 4:23–25)

Was there a sorrowful situation that did not evoke his sorrow? Was there pain that did not get to him? Was there a force of evil that would not be challenged by him?

If Jesus could do anything about a situation brought to his attention, he would. There were times, obviously, when the atmosphere was not right. Popular as he was, his hometown people couldn't easily adjust to his fame and he felt he had to leave. "They never appreciate you in your hometown," he remarked, in effect. (Mark 6:1–5) Sometimes, too, he had to run away because people had some crazy idea to make him into a king or political leader. (John 6:14–15) Nice guys stay out of politics! If the atmosphere was not right, he would simply leave. His disciples might, from time to time, have a mean streak. Once they suggested wiping out some towns that did not give Jesus the kindest reception. Jesus would have nothing to do with that. (Luke 9:51–56) Even if he corrected or chided people, he only went after those who asked for it, and he was, after all, considered a "rabbi," that is, a teacher.

He didn't want to hog all the attention either. He sent his disciples, ornery as they could sometimes be, to visit towns in his name. He told them to do the wonderful things he did. Heal the sick. Conquer the forces of evil. Proclaim peace. Announce the coming of the kingdom of God. You couldn't get nicer than that, could you? (Luke 10:1–9)

The only problem is: nice guys finish last.

And that's where people had Jesus finish. Last. At the bottom. Hung nude and bleeding before the people who flocked to him, exposed as a failure, as a political revolutionary and a religious radical. It made no difference that such charges were untrue. Nice guys finish last, whatever the charges.

It seems, though, that Jesus was even more than a "nice guy." If that had been all he was, who would pay him any mind today? We bury and forget a million nice guys every day.

They buried and thought they would forget Jesus back in his time, too. Who could erase from memory the scene of Jesus' poor mother holding him in absolute grief, wondering how her child could end up so scorned, so rejected, so broken, so dead? Who could rob of its grief the slow procession of a few decent men and a few weeping women, carrying the body of Jesus to its borrowed tomb? (Matthew 27:55–61; see also John 19:25–27)

Jesus was something more than a "nice guy" because nice guys don't come back from their tombs. They stay there. But Jesus didn't. He was raised. He is not among the dead. He is alive. (See Luke 24:1–12)

This startling message forms the heart of the Gospel of Jesus. Because of it, all the nice things Jesus did are remembered. Because of it, his death stands out among all the cruel deaths of history. Because of it, Jesus stands out from all human beings. Because of it, all human history centers itself on him.

Why? Because in his death and resurrection, Jesus took us where no one else could take us. He took us to the borders of our experience, the edges of our fears. He brought us to the bottom that looms as dread for every one of us. He opened up the darkest gulf of human terror. He not only got to death, he went through it.

This is why Jesus cannot be ranked an ordinary nice guy or even an extraordinary nice guy. Jesus, as a very particular person who lived a little less than two thousand years ago, is the revelation of God, the absolute power of God among us. For in his dying, he touched human boundaries. In his rising, he broke them.

He was proclaimed, then, by those who experienced him as Savior, as Lord, and finally as God.

Why else was he proclaimed as Savior if it was not because, in his resurrection, he unlocked the power that lets us know that we can be saved? For we are exactly saved from what scares and terrorizes us. And that is exactly what Jesus dealt with. No one could claim to be a true Savior and not go through death. Jesus, because he did, is Savior. If he can bring us through death, there is nothing he cannot bring us through as well. What, St. Paul muses, can separate us from God? What, he wonders, can destroy us? Because of Jesus, nothing. (Romans 9:35–39)

As Savior, Jesus is proclaimed as Lord. (Acts 2:36) The word for "Lord" has a lot of applications in the New Testament. It can mean something as ordinary as "Mister" or "Sir"—the way that "Señor" in Spanish can refer to an exalted or just an ordinary man. But "Lord" also has a very exclusive usage in the New Testament, coming from Jewish customs itself. Jews would never mention God's own name, so respectful were they of it. Instead, they would substitute the word "Lord" to avoid having to pronounce what they thought they were not worthy to pronounce.

It is this idea of "Lord," in the sense of God's own "nickname" if you will, that those who experienced the risen Jesus applied to him. For in passing beyond the utter boundaries of our human life, he reveals and brings God. He shows us that God is the other side of our terror. That God was acting and speaking and loving and giving in the human being called Jesus. And that he, nice guy that he was, acted with the power of God himself. St. Paul quotes the early hymn that professes that, because of the obedience of his death, God raised Jesus to the highest realm so that every being in all of existence (even above and below the earth!) might proclaim exactly this: Jesus Christ is Lord. (Philippians 2:11)

Now what could it mean to act with and in the power of God? Was this like being appointed superintendent by your landlord? Was this like being executive vice-president? Did God lend his power like some kind of prized possession that could be swapped? How could someone go through the revelation that Jesus did and it only be some kind of serendipity, some kind of cute arrangement, some kind of contract between God and his "Lord"?

Seeing behind the "nice guy" package we are tempted to put Jesus in, those who experienced his life, death and resurrection proclaimed that this was not some accidental link between God and Jesus. That the link was in the very person of Jesus—the link was in the very being of Christ. (See John 20:28; John 1:1 and Philippians 2:6)

The New Testament writers do not run around saying "Jesus is God" on every other page because it hurt their ears which were attuned to Jewish ways of speaking that would never put it this way. But the New Testament is not at all shy about having Jesus do exactly what God does: feed in the desert, forgive sins, exercise absolute power over the forces of evil, heal, demand obedience from all who hear him, and even raise from the dead.

There are a lot of things that executive vice-presidents can do, but a lot of things that they can't. And that is why the proclamations about Jesus went beyond "Savior" and "Lord" to "God" and "God's Son."

We can take nice guys, but can we take God's Son? That is the question that the New Testament leaves with us. Because to be involved in him is to be involved in his faith, to see the world as he sees it, to affirm it as he affirms it, to live as he lived, to die as he died, to rise as he rose.

And we can do none of these things unless we are committed to him, bound up in his life, belonging to him as he claims to belong to us.

With this, we are back at the idea of community, of family, of the group that is one because people belong to each other. For were we to dare to belong to Jesus, we would, at the same moment, be daring to belong to all those who belong to him. We would be swept into the tradition of those who know what he knows because they live his life.

Questions

Do Catholics believe in Jesus?

Catholics believe that Jesus is the Savior of all people and Lord of all created things. The Catholic faith stands *entirely* on faith in Jesus.

What is the background of Jesus?

Jesus lived about two thousand years ago in Palestine at the eastern end of the Mediterranean Sea in the area known as "the Holy Land," or "Israel." He spoke Aramaic and Hebrew. He belonged to the Jewish people. He came from a working family since he was called "the carpenter's son."

MESSIAH AND SAVIOR

Why is Jesus believed in as "Savior"?

Because Jesus, by his life, death and resurrection, frees us from the deepest threats to our human being—sin, suffering, shame and death—he is called "Savior" by those who believe in him. (See Acts 13:23)

Why is Jesus called "the Messiah"?

The word "messiah" means "the chosen" and "the anointed one." The word "Christ" is simply the Greek translation of

THE BIRTH ANNOUNCEMENT OF JESUS

When God's messenger (the "angel") appears to Mary, in the story by Luke, he announces to her that she, a virgin, will be the mother of Jesus; his description gives a short-hand picture of the impression Jesus made on his followers.

> *"You will conceive and bear a son and give him the name of Jesus. Great will be his dignity and he will be called Son of the Most High. The Lord God will give him the throne of David his father. He will rule over the house of Jacob forever and his reign will be without end."* (Luke 1:31–33)

This announcement uses the traditional language of the Jewish people ("King," "throne," and "Most High") to say that Jesus is going to carry on the Jewish tradition—but in a new way. As Son of the "Most High" he will bring the very power of God into the lives of those he meets and serves. His birth of Mary, the virgin, underlines that his ultimate roots are in God himself, beyond the range of human genes.

It is important to look beyond the religious vocabulary used to present Jesus and see him as well as a very historical figure, born at a certain time in Jewish history, conditioned by the ideas and culture of his world, living in the *actual* situation of those people two thousand years ago. Realizing this, we can begin to understand God as truly concerned with our history and not related to us in some abstract way.

this Hebrew term. Jesus is called "the Messiah" because he had a special task and was "chosen" or "anointed" to accomplish it. In ancient times, it was normal to designate a king or prophet by anointing him, thereby showing that this person had a special role. Jesus had the most important role in history—that is why he is called "the Messiah." (See Matthew 16:16)

What role did Jesus have?

Jesus had the role of proclaiming the presence of the kingdom of God in our world, in our daily lives. This proclamation

PETER'S CONFESSION

One of the most powerful stories in the Gospel informs us of the confession (statement of faith) of St. Peter. It is one of the few places in which Jesus accepts the title "Messiah" as his own. Immediately, however, he shows a different understanding of "Messiah" than Peter's, for once Jesus starts explaining that the Messiah *has to suffer,* Peter tries to insist that the Messiah should not suffer. To this, Jesus responds: "Be gone, Satan," meaning that Peter was trying to deflect Jesus from the Messiah's true path.

> *"And you," Jesus asked his apostles, "who do you say that I am?"*
> *"You are the Messiah," Simon Peter answered, "the Son of the living God!" "Blest are you, Simon son of Jonah!" Jesus replied. "No mere man has revealed this to you, but my heavenly Father."* (Matthew 16:16–18)

The story continues with Jesus' demand that everyone who considers himself a follower must take up his cross. In Mark's Gospel, Jesus explains the situation clearly: "The Son of Man* has not come to be served, but to serve—to give his life in ransom for many." (Mark 10:45)

*"Son of Man"—this term whch Jesus used to refer to himself comes from the prophetic tradition of the Old Testament and refers to someone who comes from God to reveal divine truth.

meant actually bringing that kingdom about through his words and actions. (See Mark 1:14–15)

How did the actions of Jesus proclaim and bring about the kingdom of God?

By showing his power over evil, sickness, sin and death, Jesus showed that he embodied the power of God himself—and that this power was for us, for our good, for love of us! The miracles of Jesus, for example, are not just wonder stories. They are dramatic signs that God is present in our world, freeing us from the grip of those things that threaten, enslave and destroy us. (See Matthew 12:22–28)

What is a miracle?

In one sense, a miracle is any act for which we cannot find an explanation in natural terms. In a more important sense, a miracle is a dramatic sign from God that causes us to either acknowledge or deny his presence.

How can someone deny a miracle?

Human history is full of those who have a need to doubt everything. We can always doubt—even what is before our eyes. That is why the Scriptures show people rejecting Jesus in spite of the miracles he worked. (Matthew 27:41–43 and also 12:38–42)

Does a person *need* to believe in miracles?

No. A person needs to believe that human life is open to the presence and power of God, however that is manifested.

What kinds of miracles did Jesus perform?

Powerful deeds such as healing the sick, curing lepers, driving out demons, feeding people in the desert, and even raising the dead. (Mark 6:53–56)

Why did Jesus perform miracles?

Miracles helped show the meaning of Jesus' life—the presence of God in him and in our world, and the conquest of God over evil, sickness, sin and death. By his actions, Jesus showed that he acted with God's power. His deeds, along with his words, reveal him as "the Messiah."

Did Jesus call himself "the Messiah"?

Jesus did not directly call himself "Messiah" because he was going to change the meaning of the popular image of the Messiah in a tremendous way.

In what way did Jesus change the meaning of "Messiah"?

Whereas the Jewish people expected a Messiah of glory, national conquest and human power, Jesus showed the Mes-

---

A MIRACLE STORY

Among the miracles Jesus frequently performed, the "casting out of demons" strikes us moderns as strangest because we do not see the world in terms of demons and hidden powers. In Jesus' day, however, people saw the world in terms of the darkness of powers that controlled people. For Jesus to cast demons out was for him to boldly proclaim the power of his rule, the presence of his kingdom.

> *"Suddenly a man from the crowd exclaimed: 'Teacher, I beg you to look at my son; he is my only child. A spirit takes possession of him and with a sudden cry throws him into a convulsion and makes him foam at the mouth, then abandons him in his shattered condition. I asked your disciples to cast out the spirit, but they could not.' Jesus said in reply: 'What an unbelieving and perverse lot you are! How long must I remain with you? How long can I endure you? Bring your son here to me.' As he was being brought, the spirit threw him into convulsions on the ground. Jesus then rebuked the unclean spirit, cured the boy and restored him to his father. All who saw it marveled at the greatness of God."* (Luke 9:38–43)

Catholics believe in the power of these forces of evil. They even accept the possibility of satanic possession, but only very rare cases where thorough study leaves no alternative but acceptance of a superhuman force of evil.

---

siah as one who gives his life for the service of others, and one who lays down his life for the good of others. (Mark 8:27–33)

THE SUFFERING SERVANT—THE RISEN LORD

How did Jesus suffer?

Along with his brutal crucifixion, ranking him as the lowest of criminals, Jesus suffered the rejection of his mission, the desertion of his disciples and even the sense of being abandoned by his heavenly Father.

Why did Jesus suffer?

Jesus died because this was the only complete and human way he could face evil, sin and death. Only in this dramatic confrontation of the greatest threats to us could Jesus show the fundamental power of God to save us from what is most destructive of human life.

How does Jesus' death show God's salvation?

Because, having died this most shameful and violent death, Jesus was, in spite of it, raised to glory.

What does it mean that "Jesus was raised to glory"?

This means that Jesus was raised from the dead and, alive with the fullness of God's power, lives in the glory of God.

Is the death of Jesus more important than his resurrection?

The death and resurrection of Jesus belong to the same act of salvation which frees us from those things that threaten and destroy us. Neither can be understood without the other.

THE HUMILITY OF JESUS

Jesus shunned arrogance of any type. He was not a snob to others and resented snobbishness and ambition when he saw it in others, especially in his own disciples. His idea of being Messiah was to serve. St. Mark relates:

> They returned to Capernaum and Jesus, once inside the house, asked his disciples, "What were you discussing on the way home?" At this they fell silent, for on the way they had been arguing about who was the most important. So he sat down and called the Twelve around him and said, "If anyone wishes to rank first, he must remain the last one of all and the servant of all." Then he took a little child, stood him in their midst, and putting his arms around him, said to them, "Whoever welcomes a child such as this for my sake welcomes me. And whoever welcomes me, welcomes, not me, but him who sent me." (Mark 9:33–37)

Must a Christian believe in the resurrection of Jesus?

One who does not believe in the resurrection of Jesus cannot really be called a Christian. Without belief in this stunning sign of God's saving love, our faith is empty, our hope is illusion, our teachings are deceptions. St. Paul insisted that, without faith in the resurrection, we would be the most pitiable of people. (1 Corinthians 15:19)

How do Christians remember the death and resurrection of Jesus?

Christians remember and relive these decisive events in Jesus' experience through their worship which relates them to his death and resurrection. Every time Catholics gather to worship at the Eucharist, they remember and share in his death and resurrection. Especially during Holy Week, Christians set aside solemn days to recall and participate in the death and resurrection of Jesus. Good Friday commemorates his death; his resurrection is celebrated on Easter Sunday. All the rites of the Church are rooted in his passage from death to life.

How does the resurrection of Jesus bring salvation?

By his risen presence and union with his followers, Jesus shares his death and resurrection with those who believe in him. The believer, in faith, meets the risen Lord and shares his life through the Christian community, finding the power to hope through whatever challenges he or she must face.

How does Jesus share his life with those who believe in him?

Jesus does this through the outpouring of his Spirit, the Holy Spirit.

How do we begin to experience the transformation of Jesus' resurrection?

Through lives of hope, faith and love, the power of the risen Lord reshapes our lives. Through prayer, worship and the love Christians have for others, they begin to experience

---

THE SUFFERING AND DEATH OF JESUS

The causes of the sufferings of Jesus are treated most subtly by all the Gospel writers, especially John. All of them reject the simplistic statement, "The Jews killed Jesus." All of them place responsibility in the hands of everyone, for our own sins reveal the same shortcomings of those who condemned Christ. If certain Jewish and Roman leaders collaborated to kill Jesus, the event still soars higher than a simple story of jealousy.

All the scripture writers strive to track a deeper purpose and set of causes in Jesus' death. All of them see in Jesus' death a mysterious fulfillment of God's pattern, a following of God's will.

John's Gospel shows a debate about Jesus. What were the priests and leaders going to do with him? He was dangerous, they thought, for two reasons: (1) religiously, everyone was following him (John 12:19); (2) politically, Jesus posed a potential threat because the Romans might use his popularity as a pretext for destroying Jerusalem (indeed, Jerusalem would be destroyed by the Romans only forty years later). During the course of this debate, John's Gospel elaborates the deeper purposes of Jesus' suffering; he has the chief priest, Caiaphas, say to the other leaders: "You have no understanding whatever! Can you not see that it is better for you to have one man die for the people than to have the whole nation destroyed?" (John 12:49–50) This cynical remark contains the insight that Jesus' death was a loving sacrifice.

---

transformation and change in their daily lives. This comes about through our union with Jesus in his Spirit.

Do Catholics believe all will rise?

Catholics believe in "the resurrection of the body" (as the ancient creeds say it). Like Christ, we will be raised in our full humanity, with all our spiritual and physical dimensions transformed.

THE TEACHING OF JESUS

What did Jesus teach?

Jesus taught that the "kingdom of God" was at hand, was coming into our world.

THE RESURRECTION OF JESUS

Trying to unscramble the stories of the resurrection of Jesus is like trying to unravel a tangled fishing line while blindfolded. There are several kinds of stories, several different traditions and several layers of memories.

Some emphasize the appearances of Jesus, others the mysterious nature of his risen body; some his comaraderie with the disciples, some the confusion of an empty tomb. Even some attempts to combine all the traditions into one account (e.g., Mark 16:9–20) are not completely smooth.

The experience of the risen Lord was so overpowering in the life of the early Church, and so rich in experience, that the disciples could not find the vocabulary or the experiences to record the power of the Lord's presence. Yet all these stories reflect, in layers, the following elements:

◇ Jesus truly rose
◇ Jesus was seen by the apostles, disciples and other followers of Jesus (see 1 Corinthians 15:5–8)
◇ Jesus ate with his disciples (Luke 24:30–31, 41–42; John 21:12–13)
◇ There were many interpretations of the resurrection (Matthew 28:11–15) and it was difficult for some to accept (John 20:24–25)
◇ That Jesus empowers or commissions his apostles after and because of the resurrection (Matthew 28:18–20; John 20:22–23)
◇ That the Holy Spirit comes as a result of the resurrection of Jesus (John 14:16–18)

What did Jesus teach about the kingdom of God?

Jesus proclaimed a new rule of God in our lives. By our relationship with him and his relationship with us, our lives would be powerfully changed. This would, in turn, change our relationships with each other.

Is the kingdom of God geographical?

The kingdom of God is not geographical; it is for all people of all lands.

PRESENT AND FUTURE LIFE

The early Christians had much to learn about the future—the life Jesus began in his resurrection. For it seemed to them that the future, the end, the transformation of all things, would begin immediately with the rising of the Lord. Was he not the first fruits (1 Corinthians 15:20) of the salvation of God? Are we not destined to meet the Lord in the air (1 Thessalonians 4:17)? Will not his kingdom come before the disciples have made the rounds of the Palestinian towns (e.g., Mark 9:1)?

It was the experience of death itself that forced the Christians to reflect on life and the future, on an "afterlife." The development of that reflection leaves its marks in many parts of the New Testament. Paul debates his future and wonders if he would prefer to die and be immediately with God rather than continue living (see Philippians 2:21–25); he reflects on the kinds of bodies appropriate to different stages and levels of life, here and hereafter (1 Corinthians 15:44ff.); he knows that every person will be judged in the afterlife on the basis of *this* life (2 Corinthians 5:10).

Is the kingdom of God political?

The kingdom of God is not political; it does, however, affect the way we deal with each other and the kind of society we have.

Is the kingdom of God economic?

The kingdom of God is not economic; it does place demands on how we think of and use money and possessions.

Did Jesus fulfill people's hopes for a kingdom?

Jesus disappointed many people because the kingdom he proclaimed and showed in his deeds was not one of power, land or money.

How does God deal with us in the kingdom Jesus preaches?

God is, in the teaching of Jesus, a loving Father who never ceases to care for us and forgive us. (Luke 15:1)

THE HEART OF THE TEACHING OF JESUS

The teaching of Jesus is scattered through the Gospels. It is presented in parables (which are short stories or vivid images that depict aspects of the kingdom of God), sermons, debates, short wise sayings and elaborate discourses.

St. Matthew presents the teachings of Jesus in a scene that almost mimics Moses—on a mountainside. Jesus gives forth his new law. We can see this in chapters 5, 6, and 7 of his Gospel. The same material is also in the Gospel of St. Luke, but scattered throughout. Some of Luke's presentation can be found in chapter 6 of his Gospel.

Matthew presents what Christians call "the beatitudes"—sayings on how to be happy (*beatus* in Latin, hence *beatitude*). These sayings present fundamental aspects of the teaching of Jesus and the promises of the kingdom. The beatitudes in the fifth chapter read:

> *How blessed are the poor in spirit; the reign of God is theirs.*
> *Blessed, too, are the sorrowing; they shall be consoled.*
> *Blessed are the lowly; they shall inherit the land.*
> *Blessed are they who hunger and thirst for holiness; they shall have their fill.*
> *Blessed are they who show mercy; mercy shall be theirs.*
> *Blessed are the single-hearted for they shall see God.*
> *Blessed, too, are the peacemakers, they shall be called sons of God.*
> *Blessed are those persecuted for holiness' sake; the reign of God is theirs.*
> *Blessed are you when they insult you and persecute you and utter every kind of slander against you because of me. Be glad and rejoice, for your reward is great in heaven; they persecuted the prophets before you in the same way. (See Matthew 5:3–12)*

The kingdom that Jesus preaches stands radically against other value systems based on power or pleasure or money. Certain philosophers and psychologists have espoused (or at least are interpreted that way) money, sex or will as the keys to human happiness. In fact, we can read the intellectual history of the last two centuries as proposals to consider these things as keys to finding human happiness and wholeness.

> "*My command to you is: love your enemies, pray for your persecutors. This will prove that you are sons of your heavenly Father,*

> *for his sun rises on the bad and good, he rains on the just and the unjust."* (Matthew 5:44–45)

Are there limits to God's forgiveness?

God never stops loving us, and he forgives all who come to him. There are no limits to his love and mercy.

How did Jesus say we are to relate to each other?

Jesus taught that we all are children of God and should show our status as children by acting in the same way as God—imitating our loving Father by caring for others and forgiving them. (Matthew 5:43–48)

In what ways did Jesus teach?

Jesus used parables (images), stories, short proverbs and questions to teach; he also rebutted those who attacked him and his message about the kingdom.

Where are the teachings of Jesus preserved?

In that part of the Bible called the New Testament, the apostles and early leaders of the Church preserved the teachings of Jesus and the experiences of those who followed his way in the first generation of Christian believers.

How did Jesus say his followers would be known?

Jesus said that the life and love of those who followed him would show the message of his kingdom and indicate his true followers.

What do Catholics believe about Jesus?

Catholics believe that Jesus was empowered by God as his unique messenger. In Jesus, God was fully expressed in our human world. Catholics, then, consider Jesus the "Son" of God, eternal with him and sent by him into the world to bring to fullness the revelation of God.

JESUS' PRAYER FOR HIS FOLLOWERS

*"I do not pray only for the apostles. I pray also for all who will believe
in me through their word, that all may be one, as you, Father, are
in me and I am in you; I pray that they may be one in us, that the
world may believe you sent me. I have given them the glory you gave
me—that they may be one, as we are one—I living in them, you
living in me, that their unity may be complete. In this way, the world
will know that you sent me, and that you loved them as you loved
me. Father, I want all that you have given me to be united with me,
to see this glory of mine, the glory that is your gift to me because of
the love you bore me before the world began."* (John 17:20–24)

Jesus summarized the commandments this way:

*"You shall love the Lord your God with all your heart, with all your
soul and with all your mind. This is the first and greatest commandment. The second is like it: You shall love your neighbor as yourself."*
(Matthew 23:37–38)

How do Catholics express their faith in Jesus?

Catholics proclaim that Jesus is the "Son of God" who became fully human. The overwhelming realization that God
became one of us is expressed in the word "incarnation." As
the eternal Son, he humbled himself and chose to relate to us
through the life of Jesus.

4

The Christian Life:
Spirit

(*Scripture Reading:*
In John's Gospel, Chapter 16, Jesus
prepares his disciples for the time
when he will not be with
them—when they will have his
Spirit.)

A glance at the New Testament might well give us the impression that to be part of Jesus' community would mean to have an encounter with him.

After all, are not the Gospels filled with stories of people who experienced precisely that? Here is a deaf person who meets Jesus. In that moment, Jesus cures his deafness. The encounter has happened.

Take the Samaritan woman who runs into Jesus at the well. He never saw her before this moment and he probably did not see her afterward. But there was the meeting itself, those precious moments in which she encountered Jesus and she was saved. (John 4)

The same might be said for the man born blind, for the centurion whose servant Jesus healed, or for Jairus who had his daughter brought back to life by the Christ who dared to say, "She is not dead; she is only sleeping."

Imagine the widow in Naim. Imagine the son of the widow. What must have been the power of the moment when Jesus saw the absolute grief of this lady who just lost her only son? Yet, in the burning moment of the Lord's encounter, everything changed, everything happened. (Luke 7:11–17)

Or did it?

What would it mean to have such an encounter with Jesus? It might take only a few moments, we might hear only a few words, we might get to touch only the hem of his garment or note the color of his eyes.

Can a few seconds change a life? Can one meeting do it? Is this what it means to belong to Christ?

Certainly a tremendous moment can change a life, but that precious encounter is not the life! We can all receive an overwhelming experience, but life continues after that experience.

Indeed, how many met Jesus, heard his same words, noted the color of his eyes as well, touched him or even loved him, and their lives were not changed—or even were changed for the worse?

This more or less shoots the idea that the following of Jesus consists only in encountering him. Certainly, we need an encounter; but we also need a way of life. And that is what an encounter with Christ leads to: a Christian way of life.

When we do more than glance at the New Testament it soon becomes clear that we are reading more than a list of special encounters that Jesus had. We realize that we have the carefully selected memories of those who first followed Jesus and that these memories form, as a whole, a handbook for Christian life.

Isn't it perfectly clear, for example, that the early Christians formed communities that met, prayed, shared sacred meals, organized, spread, communicated, disagreed and agreed, and sought to live as one? (See 1 Peter 2:1–12 and the whole Book of Acts) Which disciple finished his following of Jesus with the assurance of an encounter?

Indeed, the stories of the individual encounters of people with Jesus were guiding memories that helped people make sense of the Christian life they were leading. They helped answer the questions: What kind of faith should I have in Christ? How should I pray? What should be my attitude toward death? Can God heal? Will God care for us?

But these questions themselves arose in the community that saw itself propelled into life with Christ. Therefore Christianity was not a question of: How do I know I've met Christ and been saved? Rather, it was a question of: How do I live out the fact that I belong to Christ?

The underpinnings of an answer came with the revelation of the Holy Spirit. Certainly, Jewish thinking made some vague references to the "Spirit of God," but who this Spirit could be, if it was different from God, no one could say.

Jesus, in his own life, referred to the Spirit. But, again, he was not writing a theology book and his references seemed deliberately vague. He would send a helper . . . he would send a consoler . . . the Spirit would teach all . . . the Spirit would tell us what to say. (Luke 11:9–13; also John 14:16–17; 16:7)

The followers of Jesus could not get a handle on the Spirit from Jesus' references. The Spirit had, on the contrary, to be seen in their Christian life. This is why Jesus uses only vague references. No amount of talking would substitute for the reality of the experience of the Holy Spirit—and that experience could only happen in actual Christian life. In the doing. In the thinking. In the preaching. In the suffering. In the praying.

The Holy Spirit did not get revealed in the same way as Jesus. God is revealed in Jesus in a human life itself. The Spirit, taking the form of fire or dove, used these only as symbolic images to dramatize his presence and power. (Acts 2:3; Matthew 3:16)

For that is how the Spirit was revealed, ultimately: as presence and power in Christian life.

For Christianity was, as Christians quickly discovered, a way of life. It was a daily following, daily praying, daily reshaping of oneself; it demanded perseverance, loyalty, wisdom, courage and hope. It insisted on complete commitment. It called constantly to holiness, to the living as Jesus lived. It urged the Christian to actually do the things that Jesus did—to continue his life.

For Christian life meant that Jesus continued to work in the world through the lives of those who belonged to him. His healing, his forgiveness, his words, his deeds, his vision would be imparted through his followers' lives.

You may have noticed that this is not exactly a simple agenda. How, in fact, were people, overwhelmingly simple and unschooled as most of the early Christians were, to carry out a life like this?

The very contrast of the sinful and humble beginnings of Christians with the scope and power of their lives revealed the Holy Spirit to them.

The Spirit was the force by which they lived, by which they continued to do the deeds of Jesus, by which they were able to bring to birth the ideal that Jesus embodied. The Spirit helped them speak, helped them pray, helped them heal, helped them forgive, helped them serve, helped them be faithful. For on their own, they could do nothing but live as they always had.

Sometimes the Spirit revealed itself in special ecstatic occurrences: people spoke in tongues, people gave prophecies, people performed daily miracles. The New Testament gives evidence of such manifestation. (See 1 Corinthians 12:4–11) But it gives more evidence to the truth that the Spirit is revealed in the non-ecstatic and quiet daily moments of life, and in the simple sharing and giving of oneself in service to others. (See Galatians 5:22–26)

The Spirit, then, had to be a vital force for it shaped life itself. Take the Spirit away from Christianity, and you make it into another dry philosophy or another noble ethic. The world has had plenty of these in its history, and Jesus certainly did not present himself as either philosopher or law-giver.

The Spirit, too, had to be divine. It had to come from God and bring one to God; had to bring God's power into our own lives; had to bring our lives under God's power; had to work the transformation of Christian lives by which Christians touched God himself, and had to elevate human forms to the form of God.

Christian life, then, could only be God's life. It could not be shrunk into a special moment or even certain special moments. It had to expand to contain everything a person is.

Holiness, so we learn, is not something given at a moment but a process by which one lives and grows. As the early followers of Jesus, we see ourselves caught in the selfishness and destructiveness that would annihilate Christian life. We know sin as Paul, James and Peter knew sin.

Holiness deals with sin without so much the magical wiping the pot clean as the persistent shaping of clay into a new form. As our sin permeates our human atmosphere and our individual acts, so holiness is the sanctifying process of our world through the making holy of our individual deeds.

This holiness can be nothing other than the power of the Spirit in our lives, helping us dedicate ourselves in service to the Father and to all people in Jesus. We can do this no more on our own than could Paul, James or Peter.

Indeed, as we all need the same Spirit, so we all have received one and the same Spirit who is God.

Questions

How do Christians understand their experience of God?

Christians experience God as a loving Father shown in his Son, Jesus, and made present in our lives through their Holy Spirit. Christians understand God in these three dimensions, or persons, as Father, Son and Spirit. We call this understanding of God "the Trinity."

Who is the Holy Spirit?

The Holy Spirit refers to the person of God sent by Jesus after his resurrection to strengthen, empower, sanctify and inspire his disciples. The Holy Spirit is the eternal love of the Father and the Son poured out into our lives as power. In the Spirit, we do the works of Jesus, continuing his preaching and saving deeds.

Does the Holy Spirit show himself in special signs?

At different times in the history of the Church, the Spirit has shown himself in such special signs as the speaking in tongues, healings and ecstasies. However, at every point in the Church's life, the Spirit is working and showing himself through the faith and life of the believer and the believing community.

THE HOLY SPIRIT

Since the Pentecost experience described in the Book of Acts (2:1–12), Christians have been attempting to catch in words what the Holy Spirit does and who the Holy Spirit is. That the Spirit *makes* the Christian spiritual life cannot be doubted: because we have received the Spirit, we share in God's own knowledge and life. (See 1 Corinthians 2:6–16) The Spirit produces in us his fruits: love, joy, peace, patient endurance, kindness, generosity, faith, mildness and chastity, among other gifts. (Galatians 5:22) For the Spirit also "gifts" the whole community in addition to each individual Christian: Paul speaks at length about these gifts in his First Letter to the Corinthians. (See chapters 12–14) "But it is the one and same Spirit who produces all these gifts, distributing them to each as he wills." (1 Corinthians 12:11)

Jesus imparts his Spirit after his resurrection as the first and greatest bestowal of his Easter glory on his disciples. "Receive the Holy Spirit," he says—as he *breathes* on them. (John 20:22)

He had spoken of this Spirit before his death at his Last Supper with the disciples: a Spirit who would be a helper ("Paraclete") to be with them always (John 15:16–17), who would instruct them in everything (John 15:25–26), and who would bear witness to Jesus by strengthening the disciples who were bearing witness. (John 15:26–27) The Spirit's very power in the Christian condemns the world by calling it to different values. (John 16:7)

What is Christian life?

Christian life is living in the grace of Jesus given through the Holy Spirit. It is the relationship we have with God as Father, Son and Spirit—and the relationship that he has with us.

How would someone characterize Christian life?

Christian life has the character of a sense of peace, consciousness of God, meditation on the Scriptures, prayer, consistent goodness toward others, struggling for peace and justice in the world, and sharing in the life of the Christian community through ministry and joint prayer.

THE INDIVIDUAL'S CHRISTIAN LIFE

Is Christian life individual?

Christian life is individual and personal. We always stand as individuals before God. At the same time, we also live in association with others who are believers and cannot stand apart from them. Christians have both a strong sense of their individual lives and their life with others in the Christian community.

Holiness

What is holiness?

Holiness is a state of life in which a person lives for God and for others.

Do Catholics follow the ten commandments?

Catholics follow the commandments but do not make them the center of Christian life. If all the commandments were followed, we would still not be living a Christian life. Catholics strive to live with complete dedication to God and others, as Jesus did. Rather than simply following the commandments, Catholics strive for a holiness that exceeds the demands of the commandments.

Are the ten commandments outdated?

The ten commandments represent fundamental values; without them, we cannot begin to live a life of holiness. They stand for God's call to holiness in our personal lives. Even in the Old Testament, the God of Jesus called people to a special relationship with him.

THE TEN COMMANDMENTS

Catholics traditionally number the ten commandments as follows:

1. I am the Lord your God; you shall have no false gods before me.
2. You shall not take the name of the Lord, your God, in vain.
3. Keep holy the Lord's day.*
4. Honor your father and your mother.
5. You shall not kill.
6. You shall not commit adultery.
7. You shall not steal.
8. You shall not bear false witness against your neighbor.
9. You shall not covet+ your neighbor's wife.
10. You shall not covet+ your neighbor's goods.

Jesus said:

> "This is my commandment: love one another as I have loved you. . . . You are my friends if you do as I command you." (John 15:12–14)

*The "Lord's day" for the Jews was Saturday, their sabbath. For Christians it has always been Sunday, the day the Lord rose from the dead.
+"Covet" means to desire inordinately and improperly.

Are all people called to be holy?

Jesus called all people to be holy. To live for God and others is everyone's obligation.

Did Jesus give us commandments?

The commandment Jesus gave is identical with the call to holiness: loving God with all our heart, mind, soul and strength; loving our neighbor as ourselves. In addition, Jesus commands us to love each other as *he* loved us. (Mark 12:28–31)

What is needed to be holy?

The grace of God is absolutely necessary for holiness.

SPIRITUAL GIFTS

Virtues are powers; gifts are also powers, for we are empowered by the Spirit of God to accomplish or perform certain things for the good of all.

St. Paul teaches that "to each person the manifestation of the Spirit is given for the common good," and he lists the gifts: wisdom, teaching, faith, healing, miraculous powers, prophecy, the discernment of spirits, speaking in tongues. These gifts were all services for that particular community in Corinth. Such gifts, however, all come from the "same Spirit who produces" them. (1 Corinthians 12:4ff.)

He talks, too, about higher gifts and speaks of the highest gift of them all, that of love or charity. "There are three things that last in the end: faith, hope and love, and the greatest of these is love." For all other gifts will cease and all other virtues are for a specific task at hand. "When the perfect comes, the imperfect will pass away." When the end comes, says Paul, all we will need is love, for love touches directly into the life of God. It is the ultimate spiritual gift and the greatest virtue we can have. "Love never fails." (See 1 Corinthians 13:1ff.)

In this letter, Paul is trying to give some order to the Corinthian community. Emphasizing the variety and richness of their gifts and virtues, he also concentrates these gifts in the life of the Christian community and its good. Love, the greatest gift, coordinates all the others.

God's Grace

What is God's grace?

God's grace is his indwelling presence in our spirit, empowering us to accomplish his deeds.

Do we have anything to do with getting God's grace?

God's grace comes as his free gift. We cannot gain it, buy it, or earn it. However, since God's grace works through our lives, we are responsible for cooperating with it. Because we are free, we can resist that grace and not let it truly empower our lives.

GRACE

St. Paul could not be clearer about grace as a gift from God when he wrote:

> You were dead because of your sins and offenses, as you gave alle-
> giance to the present age and to the prince of the air, that spirit who
> is even now at work among the rebellious. All of us were once of
> their company; we lived at the level of the flesh, following every whim
> and fancy, and so by nature deserved God's wrath like the rest. But
> God is rich in mercy; because of his great love for us he brought us
> to life with Christ when we were dead in sin. By this favor* you were
> saved. Both with and in Christ Jesus he raised us up and gave us a
> place in the heavens, that in the ages to come he might display the
> great wealth of his favor manifested by his kindness to us in Christ
> Jesus. I repeat, it is owing to his favor that salvation is yours through
> faith. This is not your own doing, it is God's gift. (Ephesians 2:1–
> 9)

*"Favor" is the root concept for the Christian idea of grace.

How is grace shown in our lives?

Grace is shown in our lives by the transformation of our actions through the action of God's spirit.

How are our actions transformed?

God empowers us to act with what we call "virtue"—which
is his power in our lives.

What are the basic virtues?

Faith, hope and love are the basic virtues of Christian life.
These virtues transform our powers of knowing, imagining
and acting. They form the basis of our moral lives. Without
them, we cannot act in Christ and be faithful to him.

Are people free?

People are free to respond to or reject God's love. God's grace does not take away our freedom; it helps and perfects our freedom.

Sin

Do Catholics believe in sin?

Catholics believe that people sin when they reject God and harm themselves or others.

KINDS OF SIN

Religious and moral thinkers in the Catholic tradition have distinguished different kinds of sin:

◇ "*Original sin*" is sin from the human environment; it is what causes the *tendency* toward sin rather than any *particular* sin committed. It is called "sin" because it is traceable theologically to the first humans: that is, it has always been present in the human environment.

◇ "*Actual sin*" is any particular sin a person commits. These sins are traceable to someone's free and conscious choice to break a relationship with God and others. These sins ratify "original" sin in our lives. Actual sin is further distinguished:

——"*Venial sin*" is what we call the daily failings that we do almost without reflection, the weaknesses and slight offenses that strain but do not rupture our relationship with God and others.

——"*Mortal sin*" we name as any serious sin which breaks our relationship with God and others because of its great hurtfulness or shamefulness. Such sins, unlike venial sins, are not committed easily or lightly.

The importance of distinguishing venial and mortal sin lies in freeing us from having to think of all sin as equally wrong. Committing adultery obviously is graver than stealing a piece of fruit. This, in turn, lets us concentrate on those sins that seriously destroy ourselves, others and our relationships with God.

What is sin?

Sin is the free and deliberate act that destroys or weakens our relationship with God and the proper relationship we should have with others and ourselves.

Are all sins freely done?

All sin is freely done. We are not responsible for actions that are not in our control. Such acts, which may be evils, are still not sins if we have no control over them.

Are we responsible for all sin?

We are responsible for all our personal sins. However, we also live in an *environment* of sin which is greater than our individual sins—and which *conditions* our sins.

Where did this environment of sin come from?

Catholics believe that this environment of sin, which makes us tend toward sin, came from the first acts of the human race in which pride, arrogance and false independence was chosen over *interdependence* with God. Catholics understand this as the meaning of the early story in the Bible about Adam and Eve. (Genesis 3)

Can this environment of sin be resisted?

This environment of sin, called original sin, is so powerful that it affects all who have the ability to think and act freely. Given the inclination toward evil, we will do evil without God's help. Inasmuch as we are all part of the web of human life and society, we live in this environment of original sin.

Has anyone ever resisted the power of sin completely?

We believe that Jesus never sinned and resisted that environment; we also believe that his grace kept Mary, his mother, free from all sin (even original sin).

How can we come to resist sin?

The grace of God, lived in the community of believers, provides the possibility of our resisting and conquering sin.

The Christian Life:
Prayer and Sacrament

(*Scripture Reading:* St. Paul speaks
quite powerfully about the
Christian's identity with Jesus
through baptism and holiness of
life in Romans 6.)

W hat those early followers of Jesus, and in fact all Christians since, found themselves doing was a lot of praying. Most people think of prayer as an essential part of religion; if you don't pray, don't call yourself religious.

If you do pray, then you are religious, right?

Sure, except we save praying for only those times when we've run out of all alternatives—as the ship is sinking, or as the golf ball *isn't* sinking; when we're unprepared for an exam, or unprepared for bad news; when the foxhole gives us no other choice.

People who pray only when they want or need something, we feel, aren't really praying. They are using God. They are yanking him for their convenience. They aren't really religious.

So what do we mean by praying?

Part of what we mean is: the way we express our relationship with God.

We know what relationships are: bonds, connections, hooks, belongings that define life. In the multiple relationships that make up our lives, a few stand out as pivotal. We revolve around them because they answer the two deepest questions we have: who we are and whom we belong to.

We belong to our wives, we belong to this company; we belong to Brooklyn, we belong to America. These show the bonds that hold us together.

And these bonds work both ways. Not only do we belong to important people and important groups; they belong to us or they depend on us for part of their character.

When we belong to someone or some group, we express that by acts that further and reveal our relationship. We kiss our spouses; we write reports for the company; we walk the streets of Brooklyn; we salute our flag. Spouses, jobs, Brooklyn and America—all are, hopefully, enhanced by our acts. When we stop doing deeds that show how we belong to someone or some group, we begin to destroy that belonging. We lose contact. We withdraw. We disconnect.

But what acts can reveal our relationship with God? He is not like a next-door neighbor. He isn't even like a large corporation. We cannot shake his hand. We cannot hug him. How can he show that he wants to shake our hands or hug us?

This is where God's Spirit is so important: God's very life and love is given to us as a force in our own lives. God's Spirit forms the relationship we have with him. Granted, he is not next-door; that does not mean he is absent, silent or closed.

When God grants his Spirit to us, that Spirit becomes a force in our own lives. As God's force, we are enabled to cry out to him, express ourselves to him, be opened to his being as he is opened to ours. In God's Spirit, God and the Christian belong to each other.

As in any relationship, we don't know it until we are in it. How many adolescents cannot understand romance—until they get hit with Cupid's addicting dart. No one knows our relationship with a friend except the two of us. And we don't know it completely either.

God's Spirit expresses our relationship to him and it creates that relationship with us. Until we have that Spirit, we cannot know what it means to belong to God, to be related to him. It is only so many words and fancy phrases. But once we have that Spirit, we know immediately what it is.

In prayer, we are expressed to God, pouring our selves forth to him: with our needs, desires, joys, pains and pulls. Prayer has as many moods as the relationship. It is all part of our selves and so part of what we express to him. As in any relationship, the more it is exercised, the more we are formed by it, the clearer our selves become for God.

God likewise expresses himself to us in prayer. Some people say that God or Jesus speaks to them. Some people never hear him. Some people are emotionally moved by God's relationship, perceiving him forcefully and dramatically. Others find God's relationship less emotional or not emotional at all.

We have no right to try to predict and predetermine how God will relate to us. We don't even do this to others (or we shouldn't).

As we let another be, and be for us, so we let God be and be for us in the integrity of his self.

And in relating to him, our selves open to his self, the relationship grows, with words, insights, and song, but also with silence, puzzlement and cries. No matter, as long as we put no preconditions on unconditional love.

Yet if prayer were to express our relationship with God, in its true fullness and variety, it must include, for that very reason, our relationship with others in God.

If we each pray, so does the family. If we each belong to God, we belong to everyone else who belongs to God.

So just as surely as the early Christians found themselves praying, they found the Christian family praying, as a group, expressing its relationship to God and celebrating their relationship in worship.

Whether Jews or pagans, worship was part of their past lives. Cult, ritual, sign and hymn were the vocabulary of their society proclaiming what it was before God. The singing of the psalms and proclamation of the Torah or the prophets embodied for the Jew his collective bond with other Jews to God.

So Christian prayer was formed, becoming deeds of worship which are every bit as rich and cohesive as ancient cult. For in their worship, early Christians used elemental signs of life to express the deepest bonds with others and Christ.

In one surprising Scripture passage, two of the apostles come to Jesus to ask him to do them a favor. They want special preference. They want to be on top, to be Jesus' special people. Jesus does not refuse them (at least they weren't telling him what to do!), but he simply asks them two questions. "Can you drink," he asks, "the cup I will drink of? Can you take the bath that I am going to take?"

Of course they said "yes," but only God knew what they meant. For the cup would be the death of Jesus; the bath, his crucifixion.

Jesus said that being special in his eyes meant being bound to him in his disgrace, his shame, his defeat, his death.

Yet so powerful was the death and resurrection of Jesus that the early Christians, and all those after him, precisely used his cup and his bath as identifications with him and with each other. Yes, they would be one with his dying and rising. The cup (and the meal) and the washing would show that.

So they gathered in prayer, around the table with the bread and wine of his last meal, uniting themselves with the body that was broken and the blood that was shed.

And they said that one could drink the Lord's cup and eat his food only if one was washed in his bath in baptism. For the going under in baptism's immersion was like the going under the earth of Christ; and the emerging from the dark-wetness of the bath was like the emerging of the Son from the dead.

These were only two of the sacred rites that formed the common prayer of those who were bound to Jesus and who expressed their bonding to each other in him. Other rites and sacred actions, expanding and flowing from these, linked the Christian in a network of sacred life.

These rites still form the heart of Catholic and Christian worship. The relationships are so powerful that they still unite into one all the peoples of all the earth. The elements are still so direct that all creation seems joined in that prayer, that all the universe is drawn into the bonding of God with us.

In prayer, the Christian expresses his relationship with God and finds it; in prayer, the Christian also finds himself and his brothers and sisters.

When we have bathed together, so to speak, we can join

around the Lord's table. As one simple lawyer at the time of Jesus naively (and perfectly) put it: what a great joy it is to eat bread in the Lord's kingdom!

Questions

Can anyone live the Christian life *alone*?

Christianity is a *people* religion. It is the faith of a community of believers. It cannot be lived alone.

What do we call the Christian community?

We call the Christian community "Church"—a word which means "gathering" or "assembly."

Did Jesus gather a community?

Jesus gathered about himself people who were followers and disciples. He trained and taught them. They experienced his life and lived together with him as a group. After the resur-

---

CHRISTIAN UNITY

The early Christian Church was keenly aware of the unity to which they had been called by Christ. Their communities were small enough for them to know each other personally and for them to directly interact with each other. They understood they were gathered together into one body. That is why St. Paul can write to his Corinthian community using "body" as a total image of their community:

"The body is one and has many members, but all the members, many though they are, are one body; and so it is with Christ. It was in one Spirit that all of us, whether Jew or Greek, slave or free, were baptized into one body. All of us have been given to drink of the one Spirit. . . . You, then, are the body of Christ. Every one of you is a member of it." (1 Corinthians 12:12–27)

rection of Jesus, these people formed the first community of the Church.

What is the connection between this first group of Jesus and the Catholic Church?

The Catholic Church historically descends from these first disciples and apostles of Jesus. It traces its history in an unbroken line to the first disciples of Jesus.

Why would Jesus start a Church?

Because faith cannot survive without support and because we are created to relate to others, Jesus called people to form a community which we call the Church.

What is the connection between the Church of Jesus and the people of the Old Testament?

When God called the Jewish people, he formed them into a community. In Israel, he began the unity of all people. The Church is the "new Israel," which continues and brings about God's desire to bring all people into one.

THE PRAYING CHURCH

Do Catholics pray?

As Jesus taught and gave example, Catholics pray; they see prayer as the heart of Christian life, the flow of grace and love between God and us.

What is prayer?

Prayer is lifting our minds and hearts to God, as individuals and as a community.

What kinds of prayer are there?

Prayer is usually described as "asking prayer" or "prayer of praise." Prayer may be quiet and personal, or it may be the full voice of a community. Prayer may be in the form of med-

---

PRAYING

Jesus told his followers a parable about the need to pray always and not lose heart:

> "Once there was a judge in a certain city who respected neither God nor man. A widow in that city kept coming to him saying, 'Give me my rights against my opponent.' For a time he refused, but finally he thought, 'I care little for God or man, but this widow is wearing me out. I am going to settle in her favor or she will end by doing me violence.' Listen to what the corrupt judge has to say! Will not God then do justice to his chosen who call out to him day and night? Will he delay long over them, do you suppose? I tell you, he will give them swift justice. But when the Son of Man comes, will he find any faith on the earth?" (Luke 18:1–8)

Can Jesus be clearer when he says:

> "Ask and you shall receive; seek and you shall find; knock and it shall be opened to you. For whoever asks, receives; whoever seeks, finds; whoever knocks, is admitted. What father among you will give his son a snake if he asks for a fish, or hand him a scorpion if he asks for an egg? If you, with all your sins, know how to give your children good things, how much more will the heavenly Father give the Holy Spirit to those who ask!" (Luke 11:9–13)

---

itation, a remembered prayer, or even a song. Prayer is as varied as the kinds of people who pray, or the kinds of situations we bring to God.

What is worship?

Worship is the prayer of the Christian community.

How important is worship to the Church?

Without worship, there would be no point to the Church. As God's community, it is called to acknowledge him in joy and praise, proclaim his mighty deeds through the Scriptures, and express the unity of his life and love through sharing in the sacraments and Christian love. Worship gives the Church its personality.

Do Catholics worship saints and statues?

Catholics worship only God. They *honor* saints, particularly Mary, the mother of Jesus, and use their images only as signs of honor.

Should we ask God for things in prayer?

Yes. Jesus taught us to ask God for whatever we need—to ask for it in his name. (Luke 11:9–13) Praying to God in this way shows our dependence on him and the trust we have in him.

THE PERFECT PRAYER

When his disciples asked him how to pray, Jesus gave them simple words that showed the attitude of honor and confidence we should have with God, who is a loving Father, and showed the relationship of loving forgiveness that is part of our Christian fellowship.

In this prayer, Jesus also gave us a blueprint to his own spirituality, showing the basic openness to God which makes the spiritual life possible. His perfect prayer:

Our Father,
who are in heaven,
let your name be holy.
Let your kingdom come.
Let your will be done on earth as it is in heaven.

Give us, today, the bread we need;
Forgive us our sins
as we forgive those who sin against us.

Do not put us to the test,
but save us from the Evil One.

The traditional wording has been modified in this version to capture the directness and power of the prayer of Jesus which Christians pray so frequently.

In addition to this kind of "asking" prayer, we should also praise God.

What are some ways to praise God?

We can adore God by reflecting on him, his works and his actions. We might, for example, concentrate on the beauty of his works of creation; even our love for another person may help us praise God. Using the Scriptures often helps us know and praise God, especially when we give ourselves time to read the Scriptures slowly. People find the sacred songs known as psalms very helpful in praising God. The Church also praises God in its "liturgies" (the special word for the worship of the Church).

Sacraments

What are sacraments?

Sacraments, the official acts of worship in the Christian community, are sacred rites by which, through signs and gestures, God communicates his grace and love to us and we respond with praise and thanks.

What are the sacraments of the Church?

The two principal sacraments of the Church are baptism and the Lord's Supper, which we call "the Eucharist." Catholics recognize five other sacraments as well: confirmation, reconciliation (penance), holy orders, matrimony and anointing of the sick.

Where did the sacraments come from?

The sacraments came from Jesus and from the life of the community that he began. Baptism and the Lord's Supper were important acts in the life of Jesus. (See John 3:2 and Matthew 26:26–30.) He also had his apostles anoint the sick and told them to forgive sins in his name. (Mark 6:7–13) His followers, as part of their proclamation of his Gospel, be-

PRAYER AND THE PSALMS

Psalms are the songs of ancient Israel, written at different times in their history (many inspired and written by King David) and used for both personal and public prayer. Some songs, for example, were used in procession, others in battle, others while on pilgrimage to Jerusalem.

Christians have used these psalms not only to experience the religious faith of Israel but also to shape their own devotional life and religious insights. For instance, the famous 23rd Psalm, about the Good Shepherd, also has been seen to have echoes of certain Christian sacraments.

Psalm 23

The Lord is my shepherd; I shall not be in need.
In verdant pastures he gives me rest;
Beside restful waters he leads me;
He refreshes my soul.
He guides me in right paths for his name's sake.
Even though I walk in the dark valley, I fear no evil,
For you are there at my side
With your rod and staff that give me courage.
You spread the table * before me in the sight of my foes;*
You anoint ⁺ *my head with oil; my cup overflows.*
Only goodness and kindness follow me all the days of my life.
I shall dwell in the house of the Lord for years to come.

*This line has been taken to refer to the Eucharist.
⁺ Anointing is used in the sacraments of baptism, confirmation, holy orders and anointing of the sick.

stowed the Holy Spirit by imposing hands; they also appointed bishops and elders to oversee the worship and order of the Christian community. (Acts 8:14–17 and 1 Timothy 4:11–16) Marriage, too, was recognized as an important act of worship, a special sign of God's presence and an essential component in Christian life. The apostles saw in it a means of sanctifying the family. (See Ephesians 5:25–33 and 1 Corinthians 7:14.)

Initiating Sacraments

Since ancient times, three sacraments have marked the entrance of a Christian into the Church: baptism, confirmation and the Eucharist. These sacraments were all received at the same time and gave a Christian a "place" in the Lord's community and a "place" at the Lord's table.

Baptism and Confirmation

What does baptism do?

Baptism unites a person with God and God's family, the Church. It also brings forgiveness of all sin done before receiving baptism—that is why it is called a "rebirth."

What does a person need to do to be baptized?

A person needs to believe in Jesus and accept the community of the Church.

How does a person go about getting baptized?

After finding out about the Catholic community, a person visits his "parish" (local community) nearby and speaks with the pastor or pastoral associates. Afterward, that person begins a time of learning, prayer and discussion which leads to the decision to be baptized.

What is this period called?

This preparatory period before baptism is called the "catechumenate."

What is a sponsor?

A sponsor (or "godparent") is one who supports someone in baptism. This person represents the support of the whole Christian family as someone enters the Church.

WORDS FROM THE RITE OF BAPTISM

Blessing of Baptismal Water

Father, look now with love upon your Church and unseal for it the fountain of baptism. By the powers of the Spirit give to the water of this font the grace of your Son.

You created man in your own likeness: cleanse him from sin in a new birth to innocence by water and the Spirit.

We ask you, Father, with your Son, to send the Holy Spirit upon the waters of this font.

May all who are buried with Christ in the death of baptism rise also with him to newness of life. We ask this through Christ our Lord. Amen.

The Baptismal Promises

Do you reject Satan? [I do.]
And all his works? [I do.]
And all his empty promises? [I do.]
Do you believe in God, the Father almighty, creator of heaven and earth? [I do.]
Do you believe in Jesus Christ, his only Son, our Lord, who was born of the Virgin Mary, was crucified, died and was buried, rose from the dead and is now seated at the right hand of the Father? [I do.]
Do you believe in the Holy Spirit, the holy catholic Church, the communion of saints, the forgiveness of sins, the resurrection of the body and life everlasting? [I do.]

The Rite of Baptism

[NAME] _____, I baptize you in the name of the Father, and of the Son, and of the Holy Spirit.

[A formal, Christian name is taken or given at the time of baptism because names show a personal relationship; in baptism we assume a personal relationship with God and his people, the members of the Church.]

Anointing After Baptism

God, the Father of our Lord Jesus Christ, has freed you from sin, given you new birth by water and the Holy Spirit, and welcomed you into his holy people. He now anoints you with the chrism of salvation. As Christ was anointed Priest, Prophet and King, so may you live always as a member of his body, sharing everlasting life.

An Infant's Baptism

When a child is baptized, the parents give it a name and promise to begin the process of transmitting the faith to the child. The minister asks the parents:

You have asked to have your child baptized. In doing so you are accepting the responsibility of training him in the practice of the faith. It will be your duty to bring him up to keep God's commandments as Christ taught us, by loving God and our neighbor. Do you clearly understand what you are undertaking?

The minister then asks the sponsors if they are ready to help the parents of this child in their duty as Christian parents.

Why are babies baptized?

Babies are baptized because of the faith of their parents. Without the faith and consent of the parents, a baby cannot be baptized.

Can someone renounce baptism?

A person may renounce baptism and membership in the Church. Such a renunciation means that a person can only enter the Church again after making a new profession of faith.

Can someone be baptized again?

A person cannot be baptized twice. After our baptism, we stand forever before God as baptized people.

Do Catholics accept the baptism of others?

Catholics accept the baptism of any church that is done in the "name of the Father, the Son and the Holy Spirit," with the pouring of natural water.

How does a person baptized in another church become a Catholic?

After a period of study and prayer, a baptized person may join the Catholic Church by making a profession of faith.

RECEPTION INTO FULL COMMUNION IN THE CHURCH

A baptized person who seeks to enter into full communion with the Catholic Church is not baptized again, unless that first baptism was not done in the "name of the Father, Son and Holy Spirit." Instead, the baptized person makes the baptismal promises (given above) and the following promise:

I believe and profess all that the holy Catholic Church believes, teaches and proclaims to be revealed by God.

The minister then says:

[NAME] _____, the Lord receives you into the Catholic Church. His loving kindness has led you here so that, in the unity of the Holy Spirit, you may have full communion with us in the faith you have professed in the presence of the church.

CONFIRMATION

In confirmation, hands are laid upon the head of the person to be confirmed—this is an ancient gesture of prayer—and the Holy Spirit is invoked as follows:

All powerful God, Father of our Lord Jesus Christ, by water and the Holy Spirit you freed your child from sin and gave him new life.

Send your Holy Spirit upon him to be his helper and guide.
Give him the spirit of wisdom and understanding,
the spirit of right judgment and courage,
the spirit of knowledge and reverence.
Fill him with the spirit of wonder and awe in your presence.

What is confirmation?

Confirmation, the "sealing of the Holy Spirit," is the sacrament that *completes* the sacrament of baptism. If an adult is baptized, confirmation is given immediately after. Otherwise, with an infant, it is done later, when the child has begun to mature.

Who can baptize?

Usually a priest or deacon baptizes. In an emergency, anyone can baptize if he or she has the intention of admitting a person into the family of God.

The Lord's Supper—The Eucharist

What was the Lord's Supper?

The night before he died, Jesus gathered with his closest disciples, the apostles, and, anticipating his death, had them partake in a special meal. As in all important Jewish meals, Jesus blessed God, his Father. When he said the blessing over the bread, however, he offered it as his "body"; similarly, when he said the blessing over the cup of wine, he offered it as his "blood." This action of Jesus forms the ritual of the celebration of the Eucharist by the Christian Church. (See 1 Corinthians 11:23–26 for the earliest written account.) In word, we recall his deeds; in action, we re-present the blessing of the Last Supper.

Why did Jesus give bread and wine as his body and blood?

Jesus gave the bread and wine in order to: (1) give his disciples a share in his death and resurrection; (2) provide a means by which he would continue to be with them after his death.

Was this supper special?

This "Last Supper" was a meal made very special by the new and powerful symbol of the Lord's gift of himself. Still, the Lord frequently shared supper with his disciples, and the New Testament often talks of his appearance at meal times to his disciples after his resurrection. (See Luke 24:13–43 and John 21:9–13)

Is this meal a memorial?

This meal was given as a "memorial" of his death. By it we remember what Jesus did. As Jesus commanded, it is done in "memory" of him.

THE LORD'S SUPPER

The earliest account of the Lord's Supper is not in the Gospels; it is in St. Paul's First Letter to the Corinthian community. It closely resembles the accounts given in the Gospels of Matthew, Mark and Luke. St. Paul gave the account to try to clarify for the Corinthian community the purpose of celebrating the Lord's Supper.

"I received from the Lord what I handed on to you, namely that the Lord Jesus, on the night in which he was betrayed, took bread, and after he had given thanks, broke it and said, 'This is my body which is for you. Do this in remembrance of me.' In the same way, after the supper, he took the cup, saying, 'This cup is the new covenant in my blood. Do this, whenever you drink it, in remembrance of me.' Every time, then, you eat this bread and drink this cup, you proclaim the death of the Lord until he comes!" (1 Corinthians 11:23–26)

Is this meal only a memorial?

Catholics believe this meal is far more than a memorial because, through it, we share—in the present—in the very life of the Lord.

How can this meal be a present sharing in the Lord's life?

When we celebrate this meal as a "memorial" of Jesus, he becomes present through the bread and wine which are transformed into his body and blood. They are the means by which Jesus is present. If Jesus did not rise from the dead, this meal could only be a memorial. Precisely because he rose and is present with his people, this meal is also union with him.

Is this meal only a present union with Jesus?

No. This meal also points to the fullness of the Lord's kingdom, achieved for all by Jesus' death and resurrection. It looks forward, anticipates and begins to bring about the future life which we will share in God's kingdom.

ORDER OF WORSHIP OF THE EUCHARIST

Liturgy of the Word
GREETING
PREPARATORY RITES: Penance Service (seeking forgiveness)
                    Hymn of Glory
Opening Prayer: asking for God's help
First Reading: from the Old Testament, followed by a sung psalm
Second Reading: from the New Testament
Gospel: from one of the four accounts of Jesus' word and deeds
Homily: the Word of God is explained by preaching
Creed: the people profess their faith
Prayer of the Faithful: the community prays for its particular needs

Liturgy of the Eucharist
OFFERTORY: bread and wine, representing the gifts of God's people,
            are brought forth and presented to God
Eucharistic Prayer: the Great Prayer of Thanksgiving
—Preface to the Prayer: calls the people to worship in thankful praise and
states God's great works that cause us to give thanks
—Canon: one of several prayers of thanksgiving that have the following
elements:

   Anamnesis: recalling the Lord's Supper
   Consecration: in the Spirit, we pray that our gifts of bread and wine
   will be changed into the body and blood of the Lord
   Epiklesis: we invoke the Spirit upon the gifts
   Prayers for the Church
   Remembrance of the living and the deceased
   Doxology: prayer of praise that ends the Canon

COMMUNION: the sharing in the body and blood of Christ which in-
            cludes praying the Our Father, breaking the bread and
            distributing the consecrated bread and wine
FINAL PRAYER
BLESSING
DISMISSAL

Why Worship?
      Catholics worship on Sundays and on special holy days* through the
celebration of the Eucharist.
      Their worship represents the expression of their shared life: because

the believer needs to be fed, he needs the Eucharist; because the believers need each other, they are fed together. As Jesus said, "unless you eat the bread of the Son of Man and drink his blood, you have no life in you." (John 6:53)

*"Holy days" are days other than Sunday which celebrate great feasts. They may vary from area to area; more are celebrated, for example, in Italy than in the United States which celebrates January 1—Solemn Feast of Mary, Mother of Jesus; The Ascension of Jesus into Heaven; August 15—The Assumption of Mary into Heaven; November 1—All Saints Day; December 8—Feast of the Immaculate Conception; December 25—Christmas, the Birth of Jesus.

Catholics worship in the Eucharist not only to advance their own spiritual growth. They do so to show the place of God in their lives, by setting his worship above everything else. This reinforces as well the life of their faith community.

The purpose of worship, then, is to build up the life of the Church and to give witness to the reality of God, the presence of Jesus and the power of the Holy Spirit.

Many times a person will not "feel like" worshiping, and, if worship is seen as something a person is doing for himself or herself, worship soon stops.

When people stop worshiping, their own religious life enters a new and emptier phase; likewise, the life of the Church, God's people, is diminished and Christ's presence is thereby lessened in his people.

THE EUCHARIST AND THE CHURCHES

Churches across the Christian spectrum are growing closer in expressing what they believe about the Lord's Supper. One statement, presented here, represents the discussion of a large number of Protestants:

> The Eucharist is essentially the sacrament of the gift which God makes to us in Christ through the power of the Holy Spirit. Every Christian receives this gift of salvation through communion in the body and blood of Christ. In the eucharistic meal, in the eating and drinking of the bread and wine, Christ grants communion with himself. God himself acts, giving life to the body of Christ and renewing each member. *

*Baptism, Eucharist and Ministry, Faith and Order Paper #111, World Council of Churches, Geneva, 1982.

Is this sacrament a sacrifice?

Jesus made the giving of his body and blood a sign of sharing in his death and resurrection. His death was the offering of himself in obedient love to the Father; his death was his generous share in our burden of sin and death. The Last Supper was his way of inviting his disciples into the sacrificial giving of himself. The Eucharist continues this sacrificial giving as it invites all his followers to be one in his self-offering.

What do Catholics call the sacrament of the Lord's Supper?

Catholics call this sacrament the Mass or the Eucharist.

How is the Eucharist celebrated?

The Eucharist is usually celebrated in a church or chapel. A priest, who is the chief celebrant of the Eucharist, joins with other priests who are concelebrants, with ministers who will read or assist at the service, and with the congregation. A cantor—and perhaps a choir—lead and help in the congregation's singing. The Eucharist falls into two parts: proclamation and thanksgiving. The first part of the service proclaims the word of God in the Scriptures; the major reading is from the Gospel accounts of the life of Jesus. The second part thanks God the Father in Jesus by recalling the supper in which he celebrated his obedient death and glorious resurrection.

When do Catholics celebrate the sacrament of the Lord's Supper?

Catholics celebrate this sacrament every day; the chief celebration, at which all Catholics are expected to participate, is held on Sunday, the day we remember the resurrection of the Lord.

What is Holy Communion?

Holy Communion is the receiving of the transformed bread and wine (the Lord's body and blood) during the Eucharist.

Do all Catholics receive Holy Communion?

Catholics who have not broken their relationship with God by serious sin receive Holy Communion. Catholics may receive the consecrated bread and wine, although receiving only the bread is truly receiving the Lord.

Do all Christian churches share the Lord's supper?

All Christian churches celebrate the Lord's Supper, although not all of them celebrate it every day or even every Sunday. Not all of them understand the Lord's Supper as a real union with the Lord; not all of them believe that the Lord himself is present in the forms of the food of bread and wine. For some, the Eucharist is mostly a memorial of a past event. Because this sacrament is a sign of unity, Catholics share the Eucharist only with those in union with their faith. As unity grows among more Christian churches, we can expect more sharing in Communion between Christians.

6

The Christian Life:
Healing and Forgiveness

(*Scripture Reading:* Few of the
New Testament books deal with
the practical aspects of Christian
life better than the Letter of
James.)

Sickness seems indelibly associated with childhood. There are
some good reasons.

Our first experiences of sickness, of not being well, go back
to our infant years and childhood years. Perhaps we did not even
notice our illness—little specks on our necks and chests, lumps
beneath our chins, a slightly warm feeling all through the body.
Perhaps we were unaware of how often we coughed or how many
times we had to blow our noses.

But our parents knew.

"You're sick and you have to stay in bed," they decreed. And
so we did.

It seemed like a sentence at first. We tried to compare how
we felt on the day they declared us ill with how we felt the day
before. We ran to the mirror to see the measles, we felt under our
chins for the mumps. "Maybe I am burning up," we sniffled. And
so we accepted the judgment of our parents.

We had to stay in bed, couldn't play outside, couldn't go to
school (mixed blessing!), couldn't roam around the house, and
perhaps couldn't eat what we liked most. That was the bad side
of being sick.

Yet we learned a good side to it as well. We got attention. Boy,
did we appreciate attention! Any other time we asked for some-

thing, we were told to get it ourselves, but now our parents or elders seemed to run after our slightest request.

We also got some contact we never had before. Who can forget the intimate sense of a mother coming during the night with medicine, the rubbing of some eucalyptus ointment on our chests, the breaking of incredibly tiny pills so we wouldn't choke, the sweet syrups and Smith Brothers cough drops?

In our illness, the bonds we had with our parents and other family members seemed to jump out at us. How important we were, how people cared about how we felt, how they wanted us to get better quickly!

In some ways, it was only in our illness that certain contacts with others could be expressed. When else would dad stay up all night with you? When else would the sofa be emptied so we could plop down all day, cushioned with the best pillows? When else would everyone cede a TV program to our weirdest whim? We knew we belonged in such a special way as a child.

That is one reason why sickness seems associated with childhood. The other reason follows from it. When we are sick, we become dependent on others, and this triggers the feelings of childhood.

No part of illness is as hard to take as having to depend on care from others. After we have put aside our childish things, we live with the illusion that we can care for ourselves. We are fiercely independent. We've grown up. We are not babies anymore. And, most of all, we will not be a burden to anyone.

Life bursts this illusion because there are so many times when we have to be cared for because we cannot care for ourselves. We feel small. We feel helpless. And we feel a burden on others.

You mean we were not made indestructible? You mean that we can have aches and be ill? You mean we will not always be in control of our lives? Sickness then makes us depressed as an adult because we feel that we have gone backward in life.

If we are ever strong enough to get beyond our illusions, we may then be strong enough to realize that no one is ever in complete control of life, and no life process can be devoid of the possibility of its failure. Only then can we accept the care from others, sometimes the perfect strangers that nurses and aides can be, as something not demeaning, as something, instead, downright human.

Illness, part of the process of life as we must experience it, is also part of the experience of the Christian community. Jesus made illness a major part of his agenda in his ministry: healing the sick, indeed *noticing* the sick, was one of the clearest signs he offered of the meaning of the kingdom he proclaimed. (Luke 10:8–9)

If illness meant our lack of completeness, then God's healing would stand for life's fullness. Behold the kingdom, he was saying, in the wholeness that you have!

The healing that Jesus offered seems initially to be in the nature of a miracle; with a little thinking, we realize that it was basically a showing of care. For certainly those whom he healed got sick at some point later in their lives. His healing was not simply a miraculous anticipation of modern scientific "cures"; his healing was the showing of God's care for us in the crises and critical points of our lives.

That care, frankly, made the difference between wholeness and brokenness for so many. That care has power even if a miracle does not take place. Our modern observation that people who feel cared for and loved heal better only skims the surface of the level of care God offers to the ill.

If we are bound together in Christ, who continues to work through his Spirit in us, then these bonds will be shown in the care with which we address each other in our illness and hurt. God's family cares by its healing and by its prayer for healing. God's family heals by its prayer and its care.

So the first mission of the disciples was to proclaim the coming and presence of God's kingdom by laying on hands (note the idea of *contact*) and the application of soothing oil. (See Mark 6:7–13) As the Good Samaritan, in the parable of Jesus, poured oil in the wounds of the ambushed traveler (Luke 10:34), so Jesus would have his followers pour oil onto the wounds of the ill in his name. St. James comments tersely that such prayer is powerful. (James 5:14–15)

The community of Jesus, the Church, has continued that

prayer for the two thousand years of its existence. It has imposed hands upon the heads of the infirm in the intimate gesture of the Lord himself. It has rubbed oil on the bodies of the ill as a sign of the sweetness of the Lord's healing care. It has prayed in faith to God for healing and witnessed its prayer being heard in every moment of consolation, in every pardoning, in every assurance bestowed upon the sick and the dying in the name of the Lord.

No nightly fears of abandonment and isolation should haunt those who belong to the family of Jesus, because he has taught us what his care means, and how powerful his care can be for those who believe in him, who see all the possibilities he sees.

The care shown in our illness is also needed in our sin. For sin is a kind of illness.

Of course, it is not illness like the measles or mumps. We choose sin, and we do knowingly and perversely. We go begging for the trouble—that's what makes it sin. (No one, after all, sins by accident; you make a mistake but you do not sin.)

Yet sin is like an illness in its debilitating effect on us. It robs us of life, of a sense of wholeness and peace; it makes us feel isolated from others.

For all the willfulness involved in sin, it often is blind. In spite of advice, admonition and threat, we do sin; sometimes because of these, we do sin. Some have seen compulsive elements in sin; they look for someone to "make them stop" sinning because they cannot control themselves. Everyone sees self-destructive elements in sin: whatever good we think we are accomplishing, we are in fact destroying our relationship with ourselves, with others and with God.

Strangely, we feel very childish when we sin. We are the little brat trying to get away with something, the little cheat and sneak. Sin has a darkness about it that reaches back to the shadows of disobedient childhood.

And sin has its own kind of pain.

Remember how often we cried (if only inside) when we did something wrong? Maybe we would get punished. Or maybe we would just be exposed as idiots and frauds. Or maybe it would be shown just how much we had betrayed those we claimed we loved. Even if no punishment were meted out, we felt badly.

Remember, too, how often parents' love came with our sin? Whatever anger or grief or disappointment they showed, they also showed that they cared, that they knew we hurt and they didn't want us to hurt more.

Only mass confusion would lead us to make sin glamorous. It is just the opposite. It is hurt, pain and brokenness, all the more so because it is so blindly and freely entered into.

Now even Jesus' Christian family, bound to him by infinite bonds, shows the perversity of sin. Those relationships that should have been pulling his people together often were strained to the limit by disagreements, jealousies, greeds and lusts. The one "body" of the Lord, his people, could be so fractured and so bruised by sin.

As Jesus did, so his family had to deal with sin. What do you do? You denounce it, for sure. You try to protect people from it, for sure. You explore its causes and roots, for sure. But, after sin happens (and it somehow always does), just about the only creative thing you can do with it is forgive it.

For forgiveness is the restoration of the bonds that sin tried to break. Forgiveness is the healing oil poured on the pain of sin. Forgiveness is the confrontation of sin (because you cannot deny its reality if you forgive it) and its conquest (because you have taken away its power by love). Forgiveness is the healing of sin because in forgiveness we learn of God's care for us which even we will not be able to destroy.

Forgiveness is done face to face. We don't wave magic wands and expect pain, disappointment and bitterness to disappear. We don't write notes to say, "It's all done, so let's forget it." We don't pretend nothing ever happened. And we certainly don't imagine that sin's insidious effect can be forgotten.

The Catholic seeks just such healing, face to face, person to person, in the act of reconciliation. In the encounter between sinner and Church, the assurance of forgiveness is offered, words of sorrow are uttered, gestures of peace are exchanged, and sin is actually dealt with.

The only way you deal with sin is to restore the bonds that sin has broken, to stretch out hands in peace instead of in fists, to say we are sorry and know it is heard, to change patterns of life that have proved destructive.

So much do Catholics know that healings are part of Christian life that they consider them acts of worship, sacraments, rooted in the same family bonds that make baptism and Eucharist a family celebration.

For sacred too is the caring we show each other, the hands, the oil, the peace of God's care offered and accepted. As no life escapes illness, and no Christian life escapes some failure, so no Christian life can be such without the holiness of God's care and healing offered in the simple love we dare to show.

Questions

Does God heal?

God, in loving concern for his people, reveals his presence by his compassion and healing power. Healing is a restoring of fullness and life, a restoring of creation. All healing can only come from God who gives life to all things.

Do Christians heal?

Healing has always been a sign of the presence of the kingdom of God. Healing is a ministry that, one way or another, all Christians share.

How do Christians heal?

By faith and prayer, all Christians bring the healing presence and consolation of God into focus in the lives of the sick.

Are there different gifts of healing?

Some Christians have a special gift of healing which is a service for those in need and a particular sign of God's gracious presence. Many Christians have the gifts of healing that come from the science of medicine. Priests and bishops have

CHRISTIAN HEALING

"Jesus now called the twelve apostles together and gave them power and authority to overcome all demons and to cure all diseases. He sent them forth to proclaim the reign of God and heal the afflicted." (Luke 9:1–2)

"Is there anyone among you sick? He should ask for the presbyters of the church. They in turn are to pray over him, anointing him with oil in the Name of the Lord. This prayer, uttered in faith, will reclaim the one who is ill and the Lord will restore him to health." (James 5:14–15)

From the Rite of Anointing
After the priest has read from the scriptures, imposed hands and praised God for the wonder of his healing, he anoints the forehead and hands of the sick person, saying:

Through this holy anointing,
may the Lord in his goodness
strengthen you by the grace
of the Holy Spirit.
May the Lord, who frees you from sin,
save you and raise you up. Amen.

the ministry of healing that is the sacrament of anointing of the sick.

What is the sacrament of anointing of the sick?

In this sacrament, priests and bishops lay their hands on the head of the sick person, pray for healing, and anoint the forehead and hands with oil as a sign of God's healing and consolation.

When is this sacrament celebrated?

Whenever a person is gravely ill or severely upset, this sacrament should be celebrated. Because it is a sacrament of healing, we should celebrate the sacrament of anointing before the onset of a terminal illness.

What kind of healing comes from this sacrament?

Healing of body through the sign of anointing, healing of emotions through the consoling prayer of the Church, and healing of spirit through the forgiveness of sins.

Is this sacrament also known as "the last rites"?

This sacrament was once called the "last rites"; however, it was always a prayer for and a sign of healing. Its use as a "last rite" at the moment of death fulfilled only a *part* of its meaning. This sacrament means far more than preparation for death. It heals; it restores.

RECONCILIATION AND HEALING

Is there spiritual healing?

Spiritual healing, one of the most important kinds of healing, consists in reconciliation with oneself, others and God through forgiveness. Jesus lived to show us the powerful force of this kind of healing.

How are sins forgiven?

The mercy of God, shown and present in the death and resurrection of Jesus, is the means of sin's forgiveness. This event at once revealed and conquered evil. This forgiveness is shown, however, in our actual relationship with God and our relationships with others. The reconciliation is celebrated by the Church in the sacrament of reconciliation which heals our relationships with ourselves, others, the Christian community, and God.

How does sin affect others?

All sin is a breaking of relationships with others and with God. Even our so-called private sins affect others because they affect the way we see ourselves.

FORGIVENESS IN THE NEW TESTAMENT

The New Testament has many words, and ways, of forgiveness.

◇ *"Then Peter came up and asked Jesus, 'Lord, when my brother wrongs me, how often must I forgive him? Seven times?' 'No,' Jesus replied, 'not seven times; I say, seventy times seven times.' " (Matthew 18:21–22)*

◇ *"If your brother should commit some wrong against you, go and point out his fault, but keep it between the two of you. If he listens to you, you will have won your brother over. If he does not listen, summon another, so that every case may stand on the word of two or three witnesses. If he ignores them, refer it to the church. If he ignores even the church, then treat him as you would a Gentile or tax collector [i.e., an outcast]. I assure you, whatever you declare bound on earth shall be bound in heaven, and whatever you declare loosed on earth shall be held loosed in heaven."* (Matthew 18:15–18)

◇ *"Then Jesus breathed on them and said: 'Receive the Holy Spirit. If you forgive men's sins, they are forgiven them. If you hold them bound, they are held bound.' " (John 20:22–23)*

◇ To the Corinthian having sexual relations with his stepmother, St. Paul urges the church to take action; he writes: *"United with you and empowered by the Lord Jesus, I hand him over to Satan for the destruction of his flesh, so that his spirit may be saved on the day of the Lord."* (1 Corinthians 5:4–5) But, acknowledging how the community has been affected and needs to reconcile, he writes to the Corinthian church later on: *"If anyone has given offense, he has hurt not only me, but in some measure, to say no more, every one of you. The punishment already inflicted by the majority on such a one is enough; you should now relent and support him so that he may not be crushed by too great a weight of sorrow. I therefore beg you to reaffirm your love for him."* (2 Corinthians 2:5–8)

◇ *"If we say, 'We are free of the guilt of sin,' we deceive ourselves; the truth is not to be found in us. But if we acknowledge our sins, he who is just can be trusted to forgive our sins and cleanse us from every wrong. If we say, 'We have never sinned,' we make him a liar and his word finds no place in us." (1 John 1:8–10)*

There will always be failings from our Christian ideals and likewise conflict in the Church. The early Christians, and all Christians, have developed ways to resolve conflict and, owning up to failings, seek peace and reconciliation.

In the history of the Church, there have been many forms of reconciliation after sin: public confession and penance—once in a lifetime!—in the early Church, private confession to the abbot which developed in Ireland (with the saying of prayers and doing of penance as a corrective to sin), and the gradual adaptation of this Irish form throughout all Western Christianity in the Middle Ages to become the common practice of "going to confession" that Catholics (and some Protestants) do today.

Did the apostles forgive sins?

After the resurrection of Jesus, the apostles and all the early Christian communities practiced the forgiveness of sins in many ways: baptism celebrated the forgiveness of all sin and the person's newness of life in God; after baptism, ways of resolving offenses, scandals, arguments and the effects of sin were set up by the apostles and their early communities.

Why did the early Church forgive sins?

The earliest Christians knew, following upon the example of Jesus, the social and personal consequences of sin. Sin not only affected the individual, it also damaged the Christian family. They knew that Christian community depended on the quality of forgiveness.

What are the ingredients in reconciliation and forgiveness?

In all the forms that reconciliation has taken in the Christian history, forgiveness has always entailed (1) a change of heart, (2) an acknowledgement of sinfulness, (3) some public gesture of reconciliation with others in the community, and (4) an intention not to return to sin.

Do Catholics practice reconciliation today?

In the sacrament of reconciliation, Catholics celebrate the mercy of God in their lives in the assurance of his forgiveness and the peace we have with our brothers and sisters in Christ.

What are the rites of reconciliation and healing?

As a group, Christians acknowledge their sinfulness and common need of mercy, using the Scriptures and praying together. *Individually,* Catholics confess their sins and celebrate the sacrament of reconciliation with a priest. In extraordinary circumstances, when it is not possible for large groups to confess their sins individually, the Church celebrates a rite of communal forgiveness.

What happens when an individual confesses sin?

Those who acknowledge their sinfulness and experience a change of heart approach a priest who, in representing Christ, celebrates the spiritual healing of the Lord and gives "absolution" of sin.

What is "absolution" of sin?

"Absolution" is the prayer by which the minister shows the penitent the mercy of God. It gives assurance of God's forgiveness.

Is confession always confidential?

All confession of sin is bound by the "seal of confession" which means that nothing confessed may ever be revealed or used outside the relationship of confession.

How often do people confess their sins?

Christians confess their sins whenever they recognize that they have sinned seriously and are in need of healing. They often confess less serious sins that form regular patterns of weakness that also need healing.

Must a person confess?

When someone has sinned seriously, he or she confesses before sharing in the Eucharist. Just as one's sin has hurt the Christian family, so one's reconciliation restores its wholeness.

HOW TO GO TO CONFESSION

1. Examine your conscience—i.e., review your obligations, your relationships, your commitments, your goals and ideals and try to understand them from the point of view of your faith; understand not only your failings, but the patterns and causes of your failings; understand, too, and rejoice in your successes.

2. Decide if you are ready to change your life, if you intend to place these failings behind you. Remember, you are not trying to predict the future ("*I will never do this again*") but make the future ("*I intend to put this sin out of my life*").

3. Confess your sins sincerely and openly to a priest, the representative of the Christian community. He will greet you. He will read from the Scriptures, helping you know the mercy of God. You should confess in few and simple words. Details are not needed unless they change what you are confessing (to steal an apple is different than robbing a bank); confess the number of times a sin was committed when it makes sense to do so (you do not have to remember *exactly* the number of times you lost your temper on the way to work); you should include sincere sorrow for all the sins you have committed.

4. The priest will give you advice, trying to help you in your resolve. He will give a "penance" (prayers, acts or something to read) to help you be clear about your change of life. This penance may be done any time before your next confession.

5. Say a prayer of sorrow for your sin. Remember, your "sorrow" is not necessarily emotional or psychological since we may not "feel" sorry but may still truly intend to change our lives. For some sins, it may take years to "feel" sorrow. Such a prayer of sorrow may be as simple as:

   Father, I have sinned. Please forgive me. With your help, I will not sin again.

6. Hear the words of "absolution" from the priest; they are pronounced with the priest's hand raised over our head or sometimes with his hands imposed on our head:*

   God, the Father of mercy, through the death and resurrection of his Son, has reconciled the world to himself and sent the Holy Spirit on us for the forgiveness of sins. Through the ministry of the Church, may the Lord grant you pardon and peace. And I absolve you from your sins, in the name of the Father, and of the Son, and of the Holy Spirit. Amen.

*Extending the hands over, or onto, the head of a person is a sign of reconciliation and peace.

Why do Catholics confess to a priest?

As a sign of the public nature of both sin and reconciliation, Catholics confess to an official representative of the Church community, a priest.

Can God forgive sins outside the sacrament of reconciliation?

God can forgive all sin. The sacrament of reconciliation is a clear sign and means of God's forgiveness by which we can know his healing presence and peace. God's forgiveness is offered to all who sincerely turn to him and change their hearts.

Can someone be forgiven who intends to sin again or is not truly sorry?

No sin can be forgiven if there is not true sorrow and a true intention to follow a new direction in life.

7

Christian Life:
Ministering to Others

(*Scripture Reading:* Many of the
issues of ministering to others were
touched on by St. Paul in his
Letters to Timothy and Titus.)

A ny community, any human system in which people grow
and mature, needs its role-models.

How, after all, do people grow? What patterns do they absorb, what skills acquire, what goals pursue, what values live? These are enormously difficult things to find out on our own; how much experience does it take just to begin realizing that these are important issues, let alone answer them?

We could, on our own, figure that life is a question of experiencing the greatest pleasure and avoiding the least pain. In fact, many people probably conclude just that. The price for this conclusion is high, however. The pleasures get harder and harder to sustain and the pain grows in proportion. It takes a long time to understand that we do not live for pleasure, but that pleasure comes from living as we should.

Role-models perform the invaluable service of short-cutting the whole issue by showing us living people whose lives are at least lessons for us. Because we cannot experience everything, and we would kill ourselves if we tried, we learn from the experiences of others. From the experiences of those we consider successful, we discover patterns that we might be able to make our own.

Following a role-model is not just parroting an action, a kind of monkey-see-monkey-do system. Imitation may say something about flattery but it cannot maintain itself over the long haul. We can put on a good act for a day or week; more than that, we have to be mindless to keep the pretense up.

So part of the human and growing project seems to be discovering role-models that help reflect patterns that are successful, beautiful, life-giving and able to be lived out. (Why would we pursue something that was, in principle, unable to be done?)

As children we had our models—and we had our future patterns one after the other: a policeman one day, a baseball pitcher the next; Superman or Superwoman, Donald Duck or Little Orphan Annie; we imagined ourselves rich or powerful; we imagined ourselves profoundly loved. I will be a mommy, I will be a daddy, we thought.

Slowly these patterns got sifted out, most of them ending up in the scrap-yard of fantasies. Some hung on, either as goals we would try or goals we wished we could attain. Some of the patterns became real in our own lives, forms of living, shapes of human life that perhaps became role-models for others behind us.

So the human family continued, a community linked together by the vision it shared and the patterns it evolved. Generation passed on to another generation, ideal gave birth to ideal, experiment to experiment.

The family of Jesus, living in his faith, cannot be immune to the same kind of process. For this is a family of people who grow and develop, people who try to embody the values implied in their vision of the world.

Jesus' legacy was not only his vision, nor only his sacred signs, nor only his Spirit; he also left us a pattern of life as an ideal for all his followers.

Not that his first followers had an easy time identifying this pattern. They were probably so impressed with their simple following of the Lord that they thought he expected little else. Yet, as we have seen again and again, the Christian life is exactly that—a life. Sure, there was a lot of risk in their immediate decision to follow the Lord. Sure, there was generosity and spunk. But this meant little in the long run. For what happens when generosity and spunk run out?

They were in it for Jesus, but they were also in it for themselves. Who was the most important, who the greatest, who on top? Who got to sit closest to Jesus, who got to handle the money, who got to manage his program? For all the generous sounding vocabulary, the following of Jesus could be, in the eyes of his first followers (and later ones too!) something of a clever deal. (See Mark 9:33-37)

So Jesus beats them over the head with his own ideas about importance and power (to serve) and with his own particular biographical projection (that he would be killed). Still they persist in their calculating manipulations. What can he do? How can he get it through their heads?

So he takes his cloak off and ties a towel around his waist during the most important meal of his (and their) life. And he proceeds to wash their feet, one by one, shutting up his loudest-mouthed disciple, Peter, in the process. (John 13:1–7)

We know how smelly feet can get, but we usually don't imagine what feet can be like in a farming kind of place with all kinds of animals running up and down the roadways, leaving evidence of themselves all over the street. Nor do we consider that ancient skills still did not produce a shoe that would protect feet completely from this bestial residue. Once we see that, we see how smelly ancient feet must have been. And how dirty. And how lowly. And even how shameful.

Yet this is what Jesus handles and washes as a sign of his service to them. "Do you know what I have done?" he asks his mentally numbed disciples. "If I, your Master, have done this, how much should you be servants of each other?"

In this act Jesus compressed so much of the pattern of his life: that of service, of giving oneself to others, and doing so even to the point of death.

This has become the pattern and he has become the role-model for all who are baptized in him. Serving is an essential part of Christian life. Christians cannot live for themselves without being untrue to the pattern of their Lord. Christians must live for others.

This pattern has shaped the family of Jesus in many remarkable ways. The heroic deeds that flowed from the earliest followers of Jesus, after the coming of the Spirit, only impressed the pattern more strongly.

Established ways of life became means of seeking to serve the Lord and his people. Christians gathered together to better seek God's will and serve. Communities of Christians were formed to dedicate themselves for special purposes.

Yet the ordinary structures of life were not untouched by the pattern. Marriage, long a relationship of convenience between families or tribes, was interpreted according to the pattern of loving service: husbands loving wives, wives loving husbands, and both serving the needs of their children who grew up in the same pattern.

Both in and out of the Christian community, the influence of this pattern has been exerted. Christians served each other in specialized and general roles, as ministers in the Church, whether married or single. Christians also served the world, the non-Christian secular sphere, with the devotion of the Lord.

Certainly the pattern has not always been followed and certainly Christians have reverted back, during their history, to trying to make religion into a system of calculating manipulation. Perhaps no more than today has the pattern been tested, as we witness people abandoning the service of others, living for themselves, trying to find the greatest pleasure and the least pain. Not only are rectors' homes empty; family homes are empty too, as marriages collapse as quickly as special religious vocations.

But the pattern endures in the sacred ways of life that Christians undertake, and continue to undertake, and Catholics consecrate by religious vow and by sacrament. The pattern endures and can no more be eradicated than can the life and work of the Lord himself.

The Catholic sees Jesus as role-model for every life, the simplest and most obscure to the grandest and most publicized. For every life is called to be one of service, every life is putty to be shaped by the pattern of the Lord who came, as he puts it, not to be served but to serve, and to give his life as a ransom for many—so that many can find life by giving themselves in service to all. (Mark 10:45)

Questions

What is ministry?

Ministry is service to others in Christ.

Are there many kinds of ministry?

In addition to the many ways of serving others in Christ, there are also many *ways of life* that are centered around Christian service.

What do we call these ways of life that serve others in Christ?

We call these ways of life "vocations" because they arise from the personal invitation (calling) of God perceived in the needs of others.

MINISTRY AND CALLING

St. Peter's first letter talks about ministry as it was known and practiced in his early church community. This ministry is based on the sacred life of the community.

> "Be mutually hospitable without complaining. As generous distributors of God's manifold grace, put your gifts at the service of one another, each in the measure he has received. The one who speaks is to deliver God's message. The one who serves is to do it with the strength provided by God. Thus, in all of you, God is to be glorified through Jesus Christ: to him be glory and dominion through the ages. Amen." (1 Peter 4:9–11)

This does not stop Peter from speaking more "deeply" and "mystically" of the call that has been received. For example, he refers to the community as "a holy priesthood, offering spiritual sacrifices to God through Jesus Christ." (1 Peter 2:5)

> All who are baptized are "chosen according to the foreknowledge of God the Father, consecrated by the Spirit to a life of obedience to Jesus Christ and purification with his blood." (1 Peter 1:2)

Do many people have vocations?

Everyone has a vocation; everyone receives an invitation to serve others in Christ. Similarly, everyone who has received baptism and confirmation is called to be a minister.

Where does the calling to serve others come from?

From Jesus whose life of service is the model of all those who have been baptized in him. These calls are given form in the Church where they are exercised and authenticated.

What is the motivation to serve others?

The needs of others and the desire to make the love of God evident in the modern world motivate Christians to serve others. A sense of pride or self-satisfaction are inferior motives for serving others in Christ.

What helps do we have in serving others?

We not only have the example of Jesus, we also have the power of his Spirit present in our lives. The sacrament of confirmation (which completes baptism) specifically empowers us with the Spirit of Jesus, enabling us to act as he did. We have the support of others as well, and the tradition of those holy men and women who gave their lives to serve others, and the sacraments of matrimony and holy orders.

What are the goals of Christian ministry?

Ministry works to help people know their dignity as sons and daughters of God. It not only proclaims God and his kingdom; it proclaims the human person as loved and saved by God.

Is ministry only spiritual?

Ministry is spiritual because it flows from the Holy Spirit. But ministry serves the whole human person: mind, body and spirit. Ministry furthers Jesus' redemption—a redemption of the whole human being.

THE CALL OF MATTHEW

"As Jesus moved on, he saw a man named Matthew at his post where taxes were collected. He said to him, 'Follow me.' Matthew got up and followed him." (Matthew 9:9)

ON FOLLOWING JESUS

"Seeing the people crowd around him, Jesus gave orders to cross to the other shore. A scribe approached him and said, 'Teacher, wherever you go, I will come after you.' Jesus said to him 'The foxes have lairs, the birds in the sky have nests, but the Son of Man has nowhere to lay his head.' Another, a disciple, said to him, 'Lord, let me go and bury my father first.' But Jesus told him, 'Follow me, and let the dead bury their dead.' " (Matthew 8:18–27)

ON HOW TO FOLLOW JESUS

"He summoned the crowd with his disciples and said to them: 'If a man wishes to come after me, he must deny his very self, take up his cross, and follow in my steps. Whoever would preserve his life will lose it, but whoever loses his life for my sake and the gospel's will preserve it. What profit does a man show who gains the whole world and destroys himself in the process? What can a man offer in exchange for his very life?' " (Mark 8:34–38)

What are the elements of ministry?

In ministry there are united in one service (1) our personal talents, (2) God's spiritual gifts, (3) the tradition of God's community, and (4) the needs of a particular age. These four elements put into a definite form the dynamic process of serving others in Christian vocation. When these four elements come together in our personal lives, we then have discovered our personal vocation.

COMMUNITIES OF SERVICE

Are there special communities of service?

Since ancient times, groups of men and women have formed communities as signs of God's presence in the world and as a means of serving others in Christ.

What kinds of communities have been formed?

Basically, two kinds: communities that concentrate on spiritual growth through prayer, and communities of active involvement in the lives of people.

Are these kinds of communities exclusive?

Not really. In all these communities some forms of contemplation and action are present.

What makes these communities of service different?

People who join these communities usually live together according to an understood agreement that says what is expected of each member in terms of that community's basic way of life.

How do the communities express these agreements?

Members of these communities make promises or vows which make a structure for their living together. These vows entail the renunciation of the pursuit of wealth, power or sexual partnership.

What do you call these communities?

These communities are called orders or religious institutes or communities of the apostolic life.

What advantages come from living in communities like these?

Members of these communities are able to join with other people who have similar commitments and, by the union, bring about goals that, individually, could not be done. In addition, the powerful witness of people living together peacefully in community calls many people to the Gospel and life of Jesus.

MINISTRY AND THE IDEALS OF CHRISTIAN COMMUNITY

The development of ministry sprung from the life of the first Christian communities. In these communities, everyone was a minister, everyone had a place to serve. In fact, the whole community was a minister and the whole community strove to mirror the holiness and service of Jesus. There was no split-level Christianity, with some called "holy" and the rest called "ordinary." Everyone was holy because everyone reflected the holiness of Jesus in his people.

One of the pictures of an early Christian community can be found in the Book of Acts. It has to be an idealized picture since the Book of Acts (as does every other New Testament book) talks enough about the conflicts and failures of the early Christians. But in its idealism, it shows the combination of ministry and community that is the heart of the Christian approach to holiness:

> *"[The early Christians] devoted themselves to the apostles' instruction and the communal life, to the breaking of the bread [i.e., the Lord's supper] and the prayers. A reverent fear overtook them all, for many wonders and signs were performed by the apostles. Those who believed shared all things in common; they would sell their property and goods, dividing everything on the basis of each one's need. They went to the temple area together every day, while in their homes they broke bread. With exultant and sincere hearts they took their meals in common, praising God and winning the approval of all the people. Day by day the Lord added to the number of those who were being saved." (Acts 2:42–47; see 4:32–34)*

Not only these passages, but also groups of people mentioned in the letters of St. Paul, such as the "virgins" or the "widows" in addition to the "elders," give us a glimpse of how people combined an exercise of ministry with their Christian calling—even though not everyone could perform the same ministry and the Holy Spirit produced "a diversity" of gifts. So Paul writes to the Corinthians about the need to foster this diversity (cf. 1 Corinthians 12) and acknowledge the talents of all who belong to the community.

EXPRESSIONS OF RELIGIOUS LIFE THROUGH THE YEARS

Early Phase: The early Christian community becomes organized around the bishop; the "martyrs" are the special heroes who embody religious ideals.

Phase Two: As the Roman empire adopts Christianity, martyrdom is less possible; the life of chastity and the "desert"—withdrawal from the world—become the heroic ideal.

Phase Three: The desert life grows into the monastic life under St. Basil (in the Eastern church) and St. Benedict (in the Western church). Bishops, such as St. Augustine, organized their clergy into groups that shared common life and prayer.

Phase Four: In the twelfth century, new non-monastic orders evolve to respond to economic and social changes in Europe: the mendicant (or "begging") orders of Franciscans and Dominicans whose object was the conversion of others to the true following of the Lord.

Phase Five: The foundation of the Jesuits in the sixteenth century signals the rise of a new kind of order and community designed to work for a specific task. At this time, women's orders also take on a less monastic and more active role in social and apostolic tasks.

Phase Six: Community life becomes even more flexible with the rise of groups of clergy and laymen bound principally by their work rather than by vows. In these groups, the community exists mainly for accomplishing an apostolic work.

Phase Seven: Secular institutes, communities of people who take vows of poverty, chastity and obedience as religious and monks do, come into being; their life is not centered around a monastery or a particular task, but around the ideal of showing holiness in the world through influencing others in the workplace or through society's structures.

The latest Code of Canon Law (i.e., Church law) organizes these religious communities as follows: INSTITUTES which are divided into (a) religious (who live the vows in a particular community) and (b) secular (who live the vows in the world); and COMMUNITIES OF THE APOSTOLIC LIFE which, by vow or promise, strive to accomplish a particular apostolic task.

Are there many such communities?

The history of the Church has flowered with many different types of religious communities. This means that people who are called to such lives of service have many choices in the ways they wish to exercise their service of others.

MARRIAGE

Is marriage a ministry?

Because marriage brings together personal talent, God's gifts, the Church's tradition of service and response to true human needs, marriage is a ministry. It is a way of service of others in Christ. In the ministry of marriage (1) love is shown in a personal, intimate way, (2) families are formed, (3) the Church grows, (4) human and Christian values are learned, and (5) the special love of God is revealed in the love of husband and wife.

Who benefits from the ministry of marriage?

Not only the married couple and their children, but the Church and all human society benefit profoundly from the ministry of marriage. That is why this ministry is both personal and social.

What makes this ministry possible?

The very joining of man and woman in Christ makes marriage possible. Without this bonding, marriage cannot be a ministry and the marriage will not endure. This bond is physical, emotional, intellectual, spiritual and social.

What is at the heart of this bonding?

The free, unconditional and complete giving of a man and woman to each other, in an exclusive relationship of love, is at the heart of the bonding of marriage. This commitment forms the basis of the shared life of the couple—and the stable emotional base of the lives of their children.

THE MINISTRY OF MARRIAGE IN THE NEW TESTAMENT

"Defer to one another out of reverence for Christ." (Ephesians 5:21)

"Jesus performed his first sign [at the wedding] at Cana in Galilee. Thus did he reveal his glory and his disciples believed in him." (John 2:11)

"The unbelieving husband is consecrated by his believing wife; the unbelieving wife is consecrated by her believing husband. . . . Wife, how do you know you will not save your husband; or you, husband, that you will not save your wife?" (1 Corinthians 7:14–16)

"Husbands, love your wives as Christ loved the church. He gave himself up for her to make her holy. . . . Husbands should love their wives as they do their own bodies. He who loves his wife loves himself. Each one should love his wife as he loves himself, the wife for her part showing respect for her husband." (Ephesians 5:25–33)

"A wife does not belong to herself but to her husband; equally, a husband does not belong to himself but to his wife." (1 Corinthians 7:4)

Do the couples minister to each other?

Ministering to each other is what marriage is all about. The husband loves the wife as himself; the wife loves the husband as herself. Through their bond, the two have become one: one flesh, one love, one life.

How does the couple's ministry help others?

The ministry of the married couple means that all people see the witness of selfless and personal love, that society is buttressed by the strength of the family unity, that neighborhoods and human networks are created, and that children are sustained by their strong and mutual relationship.

Do Catholics believe in divorce?

Catholics, who see marriage as a holy sign of God's love for us in Jesus, do not believe that this sign can ever be broken, because God's love for us can never be broken. Catholics believe that the commitment given in marriage is for life. They do not believe in divorce.

What happens when Catholics experience divorce?

Catholics suffer from divorce as does any other group. Many reasons cause the breakup or breakdown of a marriage. A marriage can grow intolerable. One partner can begin to abuse another, threatening life and welfare. One partner can simply abandon the other. For Catholics, as for all, divorce is a tragedy.

In the face of the reality of divorce, what does it mean not to believe in it?

Those who do not believe in divorce accept a faithfulness in God that goes beyond the limitation and even the breakdown of a marriage. For this reason, Catholics are called not to remarry after divorce, as a sign of the faithfulness of God's love even in the failure of love.

What happens when two married people can no longer live together?

When two married people cannot live together, they may get a separation from each other. Their bond of love, however, still exists in the Lord. Even if a couple gets a divorce from the state government, they are not free to marry unless their first marriage is annulled.

What does it mean to annul a marriage?

To annul a marriage means to declare that it never was, for one reason or other, a real marriage. An annulment is not a divorce. Divorce ends a marriage; annulment says that no marriage truly existed.

Are children important to a marriage?

Children are the natural fruit of the human love between husband and wife. All marriages should, insofar as possible, intend to bring children into the world.

JESUS' TEACHING ON DIVORCE

"Then some Pharisees came up and as a test began to ask him whether it was permissible for a husband to divorce his wife. In reply he said, 'What command did Moses give you?' They answered, 'Moses permitted divorce and the writing of a decree of divorce.' But Jesus told them: 'He wrote that commandment for you because of your stubbornness. At the beginning of creation God made them male and female; for this reason, a man shall leave his father and mother and the two shall become as one. They are no longer two but one flesh. Therefore let no man separate what God has joined.' Back in the house again, the disciples began to question him about this. He told them, 'Whoever divorces his wife and marries another commits adultery against her; the woman who divorces her husband and marries another commits adultery.' " (Mark 10:2–12)

Marriage presented complications in the early Church—even as it does today. Two situations raised particular questions: (a) when a convert joins the Church and the spouse does not; and (b) when a marriage that is legal by pagan/civil law but illegal by Jewish law forces someone to decide its validity.

(a) Paul handles sensitively the first situation, insisting that the couple stay together if the non-Christian will let the Christian live in peace. Otherwise, he permits divorce "for the sake of the faith." His preference is for the enduring relationship (see 1 Corinthians 7:15). "God has called you to live in peace," he says.

(b) In the second situation, St. Matthew talks about "lewd conduct" [the Greek word is *porneia*, the root to our word *pornographic*] and means a marriage that is "lewd" by Jewish-Christian standards—marrying, for instance, one's stepchild. If such a couple joins the Church, what should be done? Should the "lewd" marriage continue? In this situation, St. Matthew adapts Jesus' teaching and permits divorce. (Matthew 19:9) Some people think Jesus meant here that simple adultery would be grounds for divorce. This is not so. If Jesus meant only this, he would not be saying anything new to Jewish circles and his disciples would not be showing the shock they do (Matthew 19:10) at his teaching.

Note St. Paul's terse remarks on children and parents:

> *"You children, obey your parents in everything as the acceptable way in the Lord. And fathers, do not nag your children lest they lose heart."* (Colossians 3:20–21)

If the expectations of married people have changed culturally (we do not, today, talk of wives "submitting" to their husbands), still the abiding, mutually supportive and faithful relationship of the New Testament is the ideal that shapes every culture—even ours.

MARRIAGE PROMISES

From the Catholic Rite of Marriage

The couple is questioned:

Have you come here freely and without reservation to give yourselves to each other in marriage?

Will you love and honor each other as husband and wife for the rest of your life?

Will you accept children lovingly from God and bring them up according to the law of Christ and his Church?

The couple vows:

I take you to be my [husband/wife]. I promise to be true to you in good times and in bad, in sickness and in health. I will love you and honor you all the days of my life.

From the Marriage Blessing

Holy Father, you created mankind in your own image and made man and woman to be joined as husband and wife in union of body and heart and so fulfill their mission in this world.

Lord, grant that as this couple begins to live this sacrament, they may share with each other the fruits of your love and become one in heart and mind as witnesses to your presence in their marriage.

How many children should a couple have?

Parents should have the number of children for whom they can care, providing the necessary education, food, shelter, clothing, emotional support and religious formation. Married couples have a serious obligation to responsibly care for their children.

Do parents have religious obligations toward their children?

Insofar as they are able, Catholic parents should pass on to their children the faith that they have. The obligation to raise a child in the faith belongs in a particular way to the parents (not the clergy or godparents!) who are the "first teachers" of their children in the faith. Nothing can substitute for their faith which forms the basis of the child's faith.

Is there a special ministry that marriage accomplishes?

In addition to the service of life and love, marriage performs the distinct ministry of bringing Christian life into the ordinary actions of people's daily lives. No other ministry has a greater impact on human life and the needs of the current age than does the ministry of marriage.

ORDAINED MINISTRY

What is ordained ministry?

When people are designated for official positions in the work of the Church, they are ordained or designated by the Christian community for doing important and specific tasks needed by the Church.

What are these ordained ministries?

The service of deacon, priest and bishop are the ordained ministries of the Church.

What service do these ministries perform?

These three ministries basically serve the worship of the Church, the services of the word of God and particularly the service of the Lord's Supper (Eucharist).

Which of these ministries is most important?

Because the bishop is responsible for all the preaching, teaching and worship in his territory (diocese), his ministry ranks as most important of the ordained ministries.

What is the ministry of priest?

The priest (or "presbyter," a word that means "elder") is ordained to assist the bishop by preaching the Scriptures and presiding at the Eucharist in the local parish church. This extends the bishop's ministry to all the people.

What is the ministry of deacon?

The deacon serves the Christian community by assisting the bishop and priest in proclaiming the Scriptures, assisting at

---

ORDERS IN THE NEW TESTAMENT

The New Testament uses the same words that Catholics do to describe certain kinds of ministers in the early Church; so we find the words for "bishop," "presbyter," and "deacon" scattered in the writings of various books, notably the Book of Acts, the letters to Timothy and Titus and some of the smaller letters.

Although the same words are used, we cannot be presumptive that the same ministries are being talked about. Nowhere, for example, do we have a description of a "presbyter" presiding at the Lord's Supper which is what modern priests are particularly called to do. ("Presbyters" are the forerunners of priests.) At the same time, the "deacons" in Acts (see 6:1–6) are assigned to help with tables—to prepare and serve the food!

Of course, it is highly likely that presbyters did in fact preside at the Eucharist, and we know that the table-waiting deacons graduated very quickly to eloquent preachers. We can see that in Stephen's ministry. (Acts 6:8–7:60)

The important point is that people were chosen for designated ministries—bishop, presbyter, deacon, and also apostle, administrator, teacher, widow and prophet, as the Book of Acts clearly shows.

These designated roles, sifted through generations of living community life, form the basis of the ordained ministries of the Church today.

the Lord's Supper, and helping to build up the Christian community by his charitable efforts.

May married people be ordained?

Married men may be ordained to the service of deacon. Priests and bishops are not married; married people may not become bishops or priests.

Why don't priests and bishops marry?

Because priests and bishops should serve the needs of the Church exclusively, they do not marry. They follow the example of Jesus and St. Paul. They forego marriage and its concerns in order to be available for the needs of their people. This has been the practice of the Roman Catholic Church for many centuries. Because they proclaim a kingdom that transcends the love of marriage, their celibate life stands for the fulfillment of love that will come with the fullness of God's kingdom.

Are women ordained in these ministries?

Women do not receive the ordained ministries in the Catholic tradition.

May ordained people have "ordinary" jobs?

Usually a deacon will have a full-time job in the working world to provide for his family. This is not usual for a priest. If his ministry calls him, however, to a certain kind of technical or educational work (for example, teaching or law), he may have a job in the working world. Priests always work with the needs of the Christian community in mind.

How long does it take to become a priest?

About as long as it takes to be a doctor—four or five years after college is completed.

How long does it take be become a deacon?

Usually three or four years of special classes offered by the bishop.

RITES OF ORDINATION

The rites of ordination designate people for certain tasks. The fundamental form of such designation is laying on of hands, a practice done even in New Testament times (cf. 1 Timothy 4:14, as one of many examples). The orders of presbyter and bishop also include an anointing with oil, a gesture that goes back to Old Testament times (cf. Leviticus 8:10–12). The rite insists, above all, that ordination is for the sake of the community.

At the ordination of a bishop, the ordainer will say to him words to the following effect:

> The title of bishop is one not of honor but of function, and therefore a bishop should strive to serve rather than to rule. Such is the counsel of the master: the greater should behave as if he were the least, and the leader as if he were the one who serves.

The bishop who ordains a priest tells him and the community:

> It is true that God made his entire people a royal priesthood in Christ. But our High Priest, Jesus Christ, also chose some of his followers to carry out publicly in the Church a priestly ministry on behalf of mankind. He was sent by the Father, and he in turn sent the apostles into the world; through them and their successors, the bishops, he continues his work as Teacher, Priest and Shepherd. Priests are co-workers with the bishops. They are joined to the bishops in the priestly office and are called to serve God's people.

Attempting to point out the sacred character of the ordained life, because the presbyter and deacon carry out sacred rites in the name of God's people, the bishop points out that the ministry of word and sacrament must take root in the very life of the presbyter:

> Meditate on the law of God, believe what you read, teach what you believe and put into practice what you teach. . . . Know what you are doing and imitate the mystery you celebrate. In the memorial of the Lord's death and resurrection [i.e., the celebration of the Lord's Supper], make every effort to die to sin and to walk in the new life of Christ.

How does someone become a bishop?

A bishop is chosen by the Pope from a list of names submitted by other bishops and priests.

NON-ORDAINED MINISTRIES

Are all ministries done by ordained people?

No. Only a certain few ministries are done by ordained people. Many ministries are done by people who are not specially ordained.

What kinds of ministries can non-ordained people do?

Non-ordained Christians can perform a wide range of ministries for and in the Church. *For the Church*, they care for the poor, sick, and homebound; they engage in community service, child-care, education, and neighborhood programs. They feed the hungry, provide clothing, give shelter to the homeless, advocate important causes and ensure that Christ's message is heard in the everyday world. *In the Church*, non-ordained ministers read the Scriptures, serve at liturgical worship, teach Christian doctrine, distribute Holy Communion, supervise the possessions and finances of the Church, advise on Church policies, sing, lead in prayer and devotions, and support the Church by their energies and finances.

How important are these ministries?

Without these ministries, the Church could not survive and the message of the Gospel would have little power.

How does a person get to serve in these ministries?

Through the local parish church, people are invited into and trained for these ministries.

Do these ministries bring certain powers?

These ministries, and all ministries, are for the service of others. All power and influence in the Church is only to serve the needs of the Christian community.

LAY MINISTRIES IN THE CHURCH

People talked about "the lay apostolate" even before the important meeting of all the bishops in the world which we call the Second Vatican Council (1962–1965) which "opened the windows" of the Church to the modern world. In Europe and the United States, everyone realized that the Church's message would be suffocated in the modern world if all the faithful did not strive to live and spread it.

Apart from a whole range of services and ministries that lay people provide, several have become quite established in the contemporary Catholic Church.

◊ LECTOR: a ministry of proclaiming the Scriptures during public worship
◊ EUCHARISTIC MINISTER: a ministry of bringing the Eucharist to the sick and homebound and also of helping distribute Communion during the Mass
◊ CATECHIST: a ministry of teaching children and adults the faith and helping them mature in that faith
◊ CANTOR/MUSICIAN: a ministry of helping the assembled community pray through sacred song during worship

Every parish, as well, must have a finance council and is urged to have a parish council. This means that lay people:

◊ give advice for the administration of the finances and resources a parish owns;
◊ give advice for the ministry and service of the parish to the pastor and pastoral associates and share in the administration of these ministries and services.

Are these ministries open to all?

Ministries are meant to be shared by many people. Not everyone has every gift, and not everyone is called to every ministry, but people should be invited into ministries that are appropriate for them. No one has a monopoly on the ministry of the Church.

8

Christian Living

(*Scripture Reading:* St. Paul's
Letter to the Ephesians focuses not
only on their living, but the unity
and Spirit that calls them to live in
a certain way.)

There is the story of the wizened lady who was seeking the
Church of Jesus. How do you find it? Start, of course, with
the Scriptures.

What she noticed about the Scriptures was that they showed
Jesus always hanging out with riff-raff: traitors, thieves, prosti-
tutes and the down-and-out.

So this lady started looking around the world today, figuring
that Jesus' true Church would have to be the one with the most
riff-raff, which seemed to her to be the Catholic Church.

And so the story goes of how this seasoned seeker came to
accept the Catholic Church as Jesus' true Church.

Undeniable as all this might be, this story is not being presented to pick an old argument about a "true" Church and "false"
churches. Rather, it's to get us to look at what we consider proper
Christian action, what we consider good and bad.

Jesus was certainly attacked in his own time for his penchant
for the fallen. Indeed, people accused him of being a party-goer
and a drunkard. He even was condemned under the awful ac-
cusation of "blasphemer"—as though he could turn against the
Father who was the center of his life. (See Matthew 9:11–14)

How curious that Christian faith has often become no more
than a way of judging others, of condemning them, of writing
them off. How curious that followers of Jesus do exactly what he

did not do—condemn people. How curious, too, that Christ's whole vision gets compressed down to a kind of ethic, and this ethic gets compressed down to a few rigidly applied moral norms.

Of course there are moral norms, of course moral laws. Jesus held quite clearly to them. It's just that he did not make these moral laws the heart of his preaching nor the center of his teaching.

When we think about it, we have little else in life than relationships with other people. Beyond the physical atmosphere of our bodies and space, there is a relational atmosphere of our feelings and attitudes toward others. Indeed, this relational atmosphere can affect us more directly than the physical one. A loss of temper, an insult, a meeting with someone disagreeable can cause in us an emotional upheaval far more unsettling than even the common cold.

If we consider it a little more, our relationships, deep and involved as they are, can only be expressed by actions: no one knows what's going on inside without our showing it. A laugh, a frown, applause or a boo: people get the point when we put our feelings into some concrete act.

This is exactly where the moral vision of Jesus comes in: how we shape, deed by deed, the fundamental atmosphere of our relationship to God and our relationship with others.

It has, then, little to do initially with law. When we fail, we are doing far more than breaking a law; we are destroying a relationship. And because we are shaped by our relationships, we are often destroying ourselves as well.

So when the lawyer asks Jesus for the greatest *law*, Jesus responds with a guide for relationships that calls for a complete change and order of our selves. He insists, first, that we must love God with all our heart, soul, mind and strength because he alone is our Lord and God. Second, he insists that we must love others as we love ourselves. (Matthew 23:34–40)

It is as if Jesus were telling us to unpack what is within us and how we connect with others. Unpack and read it, he says. Because the links, the relationships are all there, in our need for an absolute (who turns out to be the Father of infinite love) and in the very connections between ourselves and others.

Were these things clear to us, our lives would be lived in a harmony with the Being of God and the being of others that would resonate with our own being.

Were these relationships set, our lives would be organized, directed and challenged in their deepest form.

To authenticate this, we only need to distort one of these relationships and they all seem to go awry. Uneasy with ourselves because we are uneasy with others. Uneasy with others because we are uneasy with God.

Of course moral life, Christian living, deals with money, power and sex. Of course moral teaching deals with do's and don'ts. Of course there is going to be correction and judgment. Of course there will be failures. None of that is the point.

The point of Jesus' teaching, and Catholic wisdom, is that money, power and sex are not evil or wrong in themselves. They are made evil and wrong when they do not fit into the proper relationships we are called to have with God and others.

In fact, modern thought has tried to say that money (Marx) or power (Fichte) or sex (Freud) is the ultimate factor in life. That all urges or impulses could be reduced to one of these.

Jesus says that our relationships are the strongest and deepest forces in our lives. What we ultimately seek is God and others. Every other impulse is subordinated to that. Wealth, power and sex are merely instances of these deeper urges and stronger forces.

When we, then, try to make Christian morality into a repressive system that puts down this world for the next, we are missing the point of Jesus. His morality tries to relate our world with itself and our world with its God. It does not repress and deny; it directs and channels. Of course impulses have to be denied and urges have to be postponed. This, however, is not what morality is about. Morality may entail this, but it does not come down to this.

What Christian morality does come down to is this: the preciousness of every human act, its rich potential, its full opportunity. Every act stands open to others and God. Every act reveals our relationship, our link and bond, with others and with God. Every act speaks from our deepest selves to the deepest parts of others and to God himself.

Surely we will keep our styles of behaving even as we keep our styles of living. Some of us will be fastidious, some cautious, some bold and direct, others shy and subtle. The family of Jesus welcomes all styles of behaving so long as they are all family actions, flowing from the Lord and serving him and his people.

Questions

What is Christian morality?

Morality is a way of thinking of human actions from a certain point of view. There are as many kinds of morality as there are viewpoints or ways of interpreting life. Christian morality, then, is the way of interpreting human actions and motives from the point of view of Christ.

Is Christian morality written down anywhere?

Not completely. There have been many books written about Christian morality, and they all spring from the same source, namely, the New Testament revelation of Jesus. So the roots and elements of Christian morality are all in the New Testament, but there are many ideas and situations that the New Testament does not touch on which are part of Christian morality.

Can someone know all of Christian morality?

No. Precisely because countless new situations arise in life, Christian morality must continue to reflect on and interpret ever new things. Until this century, for example, heart transplants were never done. Christian morality did not consider them. Now it must reflect on these and hosts of other new issues. Christian morality is rather more like a lived wisdom than a known science.

How do people learn Christian morality?

Christian morality is learned in action by decisions and choices made consistently according to particular values.

CHRISTIAN LIFE

St. Paul had to deal with new Christians trying to live in a world largely pagan. In every letter, he gives advice about Christian living. To the Galatians, for example, he writes:

> "My brothers, remember that you have been called to live in freedom—but not freedom that gives free reign to the flesh. Out of love, place yourselves at one another's service. The whole law has found its fulfillment in this one saying: 'You shall love your neighbor as yourself.'

> "My brothers, if someone is detected in sin, you who live by the spirit should gently set him right, each of you trying to avoid falling into temptation himself. Help carry one another's burdens; in that way you will fulfill the law of Christ. If anyone thinks he amounts to something, when in fact he is nothing, he is only deceiving himself. Each man should look to his conduct; if he has reason to boast of anything, it will be because the achievement is his and not another's. Everyone should bear his own responsibility." (Galatians 5:13–14; 6:1–5)

Paul had to fight the tendency among the Galatians and other early communities to want to return to living by Jewish law. Many, for example, insisted that only those ritually circumcised could be among the saved. Paul knew that Jesus intended another kind of relationship with God, a new freedom that faced new situations. He ends his letter by writing:

> "May I never boast of anything but the cross of our Lord Jesus Christ! Through it, the world has been crucified to me and I to the world. It means nothing whether one is circumcised or not. All that matters is that one is created anew. Peace and mercy on all who follow this rule of life and on the Israel of God." (Galatians 6:14–16)

When Jesus washed his disciples' feet, he said plainly:

> "Do you understand what I just did for you? You address me as 'Teacher' and 'Lord,' and fittingly enough, for that is what I am. But if I washed your feet—I who am Teacher and Lord—then you must wash each other's feet. What I just did was to give you an example: as I have done, so you must do." (John 13:12–15)

The *example* of good people is essential for learning Christian moral action successfully. The theory of Christian morality is learned by studying the New Testament and the history of moral and ethical teachings insofar as they help us apply the New Testament values to the particulars of our human life.

Where does Christian morality come from?

Ultimately, it comes from the words and deeds of Jesus. Jesus gives us (1) an *example* of how to live by his care for others, and (2) a *context* in which to live by his death and resurrection. For example, through Christ we know that our deeds are important not only for behaving correctly toward others but also for the way we express our hope for the fullness of life. We know that our actions are done in the context of Christian hope for life everlasting.

What is the particular concern of Christian morality?

Christian morality is concerned only with our actions properly understood as *those acts we willingly and thoughtfully do.* Events such as mistakes, accidents, involuntary actions and fantasies, as well as things that are done to us, are not the particular concern of Christian morality.

What is the motive of Christian action?

The motive of Christian action is to express true love for God and others.

How should a Christian love God?

Jesus tells us to love God with all our heart, all our mind, all our soul and all our strength. To love God this way means to prefer him to all other things and center our lives on him. We give him our minds, souls and hearts by our prayer and worship. We give him our strength by our obedience to him.

How do we obey God?

We obey God by following him through the judgments of our conscience.

CHRIST'S MORAL VISION

In Jesus' mind, the love of God and neighbor are inseparably linked precisely because our relationship with God determines our relationship with others. Morality springs from the basic insights we have into ourselves as we stand before God. Jesus teaches:

> "Do to others what you would have them do to you. If you love those who love you, what credit is that to you? Even sinners love those who love them. If you do good to those who do good to you, how can you claim any credit? Sinners do as much. If you lend to those from whom you expect repayment, what merit is there in it for you? Even sinners lend to sinners, expecting to be repaid in full. Love your enemy and do good; lend without expecting repayment. Then will your recompense be great. You will rightly be called sons of the Most High, since he himself is good to the ungrateful and the wicked. Be compassionate, as your Father is compassionate. Do not judge, and you will not be judged. Do not condemn, and you will not be condemned. Pardon and you shall be pardoned. Give and it shall be given back to you."
> (Luke 6:31–37)

What is conscience?

Conscience is the judgment we make about the goodness or badness of an action in view of the teaching of Jesus and Christian moral tradition. Conscience is the absolute moral directive in our lives because an individual only has this enlightened judgment before a particular action is done. Conscience shapes the particular actions we do, making them good or bad.

What do Christians call good?

Christians call good whatever follows in accord with the moral vision and teaching of Jesus.

What do Christians call evil?

Christians call evil whatever contradicts or undermines the moral vision and teaching of Jesus.

How are Christians to love others?

Christians are to love others as themselves, that is, to prefer them with the same constant value that they have for themselves.

How is this constant preference shown?

By treating others with respect and justice because of their inherent value, rather than by using them simply to enhance ourselves.

Does this love of others have practical consequences?

Indeed, it comes to affect how we speak, think and act toward others. It affects every part of our lives. Lying, for example, is simply the misuse of another's mind and a non-respect for the other's desire for and need of truth. Theft, likewise, is an improper manipulation of the property of others for our own wealth.

Does Christian morality have an attitude toward property?

Christian morality respects the right of everyone to own property. But that ownership must be placed in the context of our love for others and God. We have no right to own as much as we want when others have less than is needed for their life.

Does Christian morality have an attitude toward the human body?

Christians consider the human body sacred and treat it with respect.

How is the human body disrespected?

By destructive and self-destructive acts, people show disrespect to their bodies: addictions, over-indulgence, lack of hygiene, improper dieting, using the body for wrong purposes (such as experiments), violence, abortion, murder and improper sexual activity.

JESUS AND THE POINT OF LIFE

Jesus' temptation was like anyone's: to put someone else, or even his own needs, in place of God. The purity of his vision, why he was living, was the key to his ministry. Jesus knew he lived for his Father. Once that was clear, everything else was clear. He was free, then, to live for others.

To the tempter's suggestions, Jesus responds that we do not live by bread but rather "by every word that comes from the mouth of God." Likewise, we do not put God to the test, treating him as an ornament of our success or happiness. And, most directly, Jesus shuts the tempter up by affirming: "You shall do homage to the Lord your God; him alone shall you adore." (See Matthew 4:1–11)

From this kind of clarity, Jesus could then judge every situation and every moment that was given him.

JESUS AND THE LAW

Jesus' penetrating analysis of the law led him to the deepest strains of human motivation. People could easily, for example, accept laws: do not murder, do not commit adultery, an eye for an eye, an oath is a word of honor. But this same law, Jesus observed, neither prevented sin nor prevented people from thinking up ways around them. Jesus wanted to push morality deeper, to the sources of our actions, to the urges behind the sinful deed—because laws can deal only with deeds, but not with the profound and subtle roots of those deeds.

"You have heard the commandment imposed on your forefathers, 'You shall not commit murder; every murderer shall be liable to judgment.' What I say to you is: everyone who grows angry with his brother shall be liable to judgment." (Matthew 5:21–22)

In this way, Jesus invites us to the most profound moral renewal, the renewal of the heart.

What is proper sexual activity?

Sexual activity, insofar as it bespeaks intimate union and love, and insofar as it begins human life, belongs in a situation of committed and stable love. Outside of such a commitment, sexual activity becomes an end-in-itself and soon grows out of control. Sexual activity should never be an end in itself but always a profound way to show love and commitment. For this reason, sexual activity properly belongs in marriage.

Does Christian morality only deal with how we treat individuals?

Christian morality is also greatly concerned about societies and groups. Part of our love for others is shown in how we care for their "social bodies": families, communities, cities and nations.

May anyone control another's moral action?

No one may control another's moral action, for that would be not to respect that person. Certainly, no government or group, not even one's family, may force one to do an act that is evil.

Do Catholics ever change moral teaching?

Catholics deepen their moral awareness, but their moral teaching, in its values and goals, never changes.

Can people disagree with the moral teaching of the Church?

Sure. People disagree with everything and anything. Catholics, however, must seriously consider the moral teaching of their religious tradition because it springs from Jesus and the constant reflection of those who have followed Jesus. A sincere Catholic never disregards or ignores the Church's teaching. Depending on the disagreement, if it concerns a very serious matter, a person in honesty may have to no longer be part of the Catholic family.

9

The Organization of the Church

(*Scripture Reading:* St. Matthew's
18th Chapter, verses 1–20, treats
issues related to authority,
organization and service.)

When we go, say, to England, we want to see the royalty and the panoply of people associated with them. This comes as part of the culture that has evolved from kings, queens and a democratic tradition!

There is a curiosity, as well, about the Church, whose tradition, while without kings and queens and democracy, has evolved an elaborate organization and various important roles and functions within this organization.

When we imagine a Church procession, with pompomed monsignors and mitered bishops, we may be momentarily dazzled by it all. What's it for? we ask. All those garments, all those official looking people? Is it just color? Is it simple love of a parade?

The organization of the Church is far more than color and parade. It is the skeleton of ministry. It is the structure which helps the Church be the community of the Lord, each member serving the other.

Behind the titles and robes, underneath the divisions and subdivisions, lie interrelationships that are the webbing of a community's life. Whose service will administer the material needs of the community? Whose service will direct the organizational flow? Whose efforts will allow so many diverse people to gather in peace and hope? Who will be a clearing house for coordinating efforts, for training and focusing ministries, for resolving problems?

After dealing with these kinds of issues for twenty centuries, roles have to evolve and titles have to be given. An organization develops to make easy the multiple transactions of a human community struggling to be the faithful family of Christ.

These organizational layers are not simply arbitrary creations of history. Nor can they be rearranged like some kind of super-corporate reorganization. They flow from the life of Christ's family as infused with his own patterns of service, of teaching, or worship and of reconciling.

In these patterns ministries and services for all members of the Church continue to grow, for no member can be exempt from responsibility for others and for the community.

Another way of looking at all this is quite simple: Christ's family must answer the ancient question Cain asked God: "Am I my brother's keeper?"

"Yes," says Jesus, "your brother's and your sister's."

We could see all organization as just putting flesh on that simple answer.

Questions

How is the Catholic Church organized?

Fundamentally, the Church is organized around the bishop who is responsible for the teaching and worship of the Christian community in his territory. We call such a territory a "diocese." Bishops, in communion with each other and the Bishop of Rome, seek to continue the work of Jesus. Bishops carry on the ministry of the first followers of Jesus by their faithfulness to the Scriptures and the worship of the Church. A diocese, in turn, is organized into "parishes." Each parish has a pastor who cares for the spiritual needs of its people.

Are dioceses and parishes independent?

Parishes are all dependent on the bishop of the diocese to which they belong. All dioceses are joined together in the unity of the Catholic community. Each bishop is responsible

THE TEACHING CHURCH

The organization of the Church exists to make easier its basic works: worship and teaching.

"Teaching" entails principally the proclamation of the Gospel and the explanation and defense of that Gospel.

The Gospel's proclamation happens at worship where, carried in procession, the Scripture is spoken with clarity, vigor and reverence.

That proclamation, however, could not be sustained without a tremendous teaching effort: for God's word uses our words. And once we begin to think about our words, we begin to ask questions, make interconnections, unravel implications and clarify.

Teaching occurs at many levels:

◊ CATECHESIS: presenting the Gospel and its implications for faith and life for the first time to a person or people.
◊ EDUCATION AND FORMATION: reflecting on the Gospel as it touches maturing minds and shapes lived experiences.
◊ SCHOLARSHIP: study and examination of the Gospel and the history of Christian thought and teaching.

These levels happen within the Church which, through its bishops, supports and clarifies the Gospel and its implications:

◊ THE BISHOP through letters and instructions communicates with his people.
◊ GATHERINGS OF BISHOPS meet to deal with regional questions and programs.
◊ THE SYNOD which gathers bishops from all around the world to meet with the Pope to deal with specific topics.
◊ THE COUNCIL which is the meeting of all bishops called by the Pope to deal with major issues, questions and policy.

The Pope, as bishop of Rome, has a ministry for all the Church. He stands in the line of Peter who is called to confess the Lord (Matthew 16:13ff.) and strengthen his brothers and sisters in the faith (Luke 22:31ff.). The Pope teaches through many letters, addresses and audiences—in Rome and throughout the world. His large and important letters are called "encyclicals" (i.e., letters that "make the circle" of bishops).

for his own diocese; even so, each is also bound by faith and love to the other dioceses of the Church and to the universal Church.

Is the bishop answerable to anyone?

The bishop is answerable to his fellow bishops and to the Pope.

What is a Pope?

"Pope" is the name Catholics give the Bishop of Rome; it comes from the word for father (*papa*). The diocese of Rome, because of its tradition, has enjoyed pre-eminence in the Church; the Bishops of Rome have shown this pre-eminence through their ministry of unifying and strengthening their fellow bishops and all the members of the Church by their teaching and leadership.

Where did this pre-eminence come from?

From the tradition of the apostles Peter and Paul, who were martyred at Rome and who had the special task of strengthening the early followers of Jesus and proclaiming the Gospel to all peoples. While various political and historical events have influenced the development of the papacy, the ministry comes ultimately from the call of Jesus and the working of the Spirit in guiding the Church.

How do bishops work with the Pope?

The bishops, through meetings and constant communication, help the Pope understand the needs of the world and the questions of modern people. The Pope, in turn, uses the help of the bishops to express the faith to people today.

What is a cardinal?

A cardinal is someone whom the Pope chooses to advise him on important matters. Almost always, a cardinal is a bishop.

WHAT IS INFALLIBILITY?

Infallibility is a technical word to describe what Catholics believe about the teaching of the Church concerning faith and morals in certain very definite instances. Precisely, the word means "free from error" and it indicates the quality of being "error-free" in certain ways of teaching, namely:

—*The whole Church* is infallible when it pronounces what it believes and has always believed.

—*The bishops, in union with the bishop of Rome,* are infallible when they speak for the whole Church, stating what it believes and has always believed.

—*The Pope,* when he speaks on behalf of the Church, in union with the bishops, about faith and morals in a binding way, also enjoys the quality of infallibility, of being free from error.

Noted especially are the following facts: not every statement by Pope or bishops enjoys infallibility—in fact, very few such statements are made: nor does infallibility confer knowledge—it rather *prevents* error; nor does it grant political power or guarantee that what is taught will be "the final word." Infallibility's quality is to say only that these teachings are free-from-error.

This term, infallibility, can be used to describe the quality of certain Church teachings because it stems from the belief of Catholics and all Christians: that God is faithful and does not abandon his people, and that the Spirit of God guides the people that he has gathered as his Church (see John 14:26).

Who chooses a Pope?

After a Pope dies, the cardinals gather and choose someone to be the next Pope.

What is the work of a bishop?

A bishop is one who "oversees" the teaching and worship of the Church in his diocese (territory). He uses the help of priests and lay people in this difficult task.

ORGANIZATIONAL CHART OF THE CATHOLIC CHURCH

	Area	*Administered by*
FIRST LEVEL	PARISH (Local Church Community)	PASTOR Associate pastors Parish council Finance council
SECOND LEVEL	DIOCESE (Distinct Church Territory)	BISHOP Coadjutor bishops Presbyterial council Synod
THIRD LEVEL*	ARCHDIOCESE (Cluster of Dioceses in an Area)	ARCHBISHOP
FOURTH LEVEL*	NATIONAL CONFERENCE (Composed of Bishops from a Nation)	BISHOP/PRESIDENT

FIFTH LEVEL	UNIVERSAL CHURCH
	(All Catholics in Eastern and Western Church)
		POPE
		Council
		Cardinals
		Curia-committees
		  that administer
		  Church policies

*Levels three and four are for the convenient cooperation and coordination between bishops and dioceses.

WHAT IS CANON LAW?

Canon law is the current collection of law, received from the past practices and judgments of the Church, which specifies the rights and obligations of the members of the Church. Its most recent re-editing and publishing was in 1984.

How do priests and deacons work with their bishop?

The bishop appoints priests and deacons to their tasks; he consults with a special group of them on a regular basis to better understand the needs of the people in his diocese.

Who else has a role in the organization of the Church?

All people baptized into Jesus are members of the Church and share in the worship, teaching and ministry of the Church. As part of the many ministries that people perform in the Church, they advise their priests and bishop through parish councils, pastoral councils and various advisory boards.

10

A Community That Hopes

(*Scripture Reading:* St. Paul sums
up the longing for both personal
and universal fullness in his letter
to the Romans 8:18–39.)

N o matter how sweet life is to us, we are disappointed. Not that we complain all the time. In fact, few of us complain enough, preferring the inconvenience of the moment for an outright battle with someone over something we would just as soon put up with.

So we tolerate sloppy work from co-workers, arbitrary decisions from our bosses, less than decent marks from our children, wrinkles in our wrinkle-free slacks, runs in our hosiery, and sneers from our neighbors. We put up with cold chicken soup and hot beer, over-priced automobiles and over-long waits at the doctor's office. We tolerate all these things and even more because we feel badly, sometimes guilty, when we complain.

These inconveniences and even offenses are not, however, the big disappointments of our lives. Even if we had suffered through broken marriages and the broken lives of those we loved, these still would not be classified as the major disappointments. Rather these are instances of a disappointment even deeper and more pressing.

Perhaps we can point out this deeper disappointment by alluding to the experiences we have had after we have waited a long time for something. Say we have waited to buy a nice new car or saved for years to get a lovely house—standard items which modern people long for and struggle for.

What happens, though, after we get what we have sought?

Almost without exception, we feel let down. As if the expectation should have yielded more for us. As if the excitement should have stayed longer.

This disappointment might be put in the words: Is that all there is?

Because we expect more. More energy, more life, more sensation, more power, more joy, more . . . something. And yet, in spite of this built-in set of expectations, we feel let down; is that *all* there is?

Even more unsettling is the fact that we can extend this impression that there should be more to all of life. We can begin to wonder about our breathing and thinking and loving and working: is that all there is?

Not that we want to be ungrateful, of course. Naturally, life is life and we'll take it as we can. Naturally, too, when life starts getting near its end, we are quite content for what we have had. Doesn't there seem to be a kind of great nobility in settling for life as it comes to us? Who are we to ask for more?

Yet let's not run too quickly after philosophical sweet-and-sour consolation, because our sense that we want more, or that there should be more, comes from life itself. The expectations we have, the hopes that we have, represent more than our sense of being cheated or not being grateful. These hopes come from our very life experiences which contain, without a doubt, some sense of transcendence.

Transcendence? Whatever is that?

Transcendence is the context of our lives that gives us the impression that we were meant for more than working fifty or so years and living seventy or so years and then being buried or cremated as if we were to twinkle for a moment and then stop. Transcendence is that context of our lives that makes us wonder why we want to know, always want to know more, and cannot stop wondering, or why we want to love, ever more deeply and truly (whatever the disappointments) and simply cannot turn our loving off.

Transcendence makes us wonder if the whole sweep of creation really is only as modern science tries to depict it: we have the Big Bang followed by some kind of hot cosmic soup; then we have formation of the precise amount of hydrogen and helium, and the coagulation of particles into gasses, gasses into bodies, bodies into galaxies, galaxies into universes; the evolution of certain of these planetary bodies has some chance for life with the formation of acids into elaborate protein chains that, under an exact combination, create some genetic material; and, finally, we have the development of this material into the vast scope of living beings that we can partially document today. Science exults over all of this—and, yet, what is it for? Is it all precisely and only so we can sell automobiles or plant gardens or worry about our weight or beget the next generation that will wonder just as we do?

Transcendence is the context of our lives that makes us ask: What is it all for, really for?

The moments that we have, tinged with disappointment and transcendence, either are all we have or they point to something more that we hope for. If these moments just come to an end, then the disappointment and transcendence is pointless jest—a trick of nature, a warp of evolution, and a massive waste of life and energy.

For if the point of life was simply to survive enough to beget, nature could have stopped with germs or worms. It need not have gone on to us, the human species, glowing with intelligence and effort and love. Nature needs none of that glow, nor does survival.

Yet if the point of life is more than surviving enough to beget, how is that point to be attained?

Christians believe they have glimpsed the answer to that in the experience of Jesus whose dying and rising have opened up the limits of human transcendence toward fulfillment.

In Christ, alive and risen, are contained the values and relationships that undergird human life. Indeed, it is his resurrection that lets him be able to relate to all humans through all time; and it is his resurrection that gives us the idea that, say, what we have come to know and love will not be just the twitchings of atoms but human achievement itself.

Much of this, of course, has been played out in some ideas of heaven and after-life. Even more, it has gotten packaged into a set of images and fantasies that include, in part, clouds, little angels with harps, pearly gates, big books and scales, and God as a very old man with a very large beard.

How human hope persists, to endure such imaginings! If this is how we picture transcendence, then we are setting ourselves up to be disappointed yet again. Imagine getting to heaven and having to remark: Is this all there is?

Philosophers who have attacked such visions of heaven claim that they are only opiate and illusion. A system to keep people miserable in this life for the sake of glory in the next. A fantasy for the uneducated that contains no real hope because life continues in its dreary present.

Yet this is precisely where the brilliance of Christian hope comes in: that the resurrection of the Lord points both to this present world and whatever life that will follow.

It is not as though Jesus rose to escape us. He rose to be present to us and empower us with his very life and Spirit. And the verification that he claimed for his resurrection is the transformation of human life, value and hope through the service of those who follow him. Jesus offered no pie-in-the-sky without bread on this earth as well.

For Catholic life this is a two-focused hoping: for ultimate transcendence in life unending and for the transcendence of peace, justice and full life for all the world. It makes no sense to hope for life everlasting if we have perverted the very meaning of life in this world by deeds of death, deceit, manipulation and despair.

The double focus of Catholic hope is not like crossed-eyes that see two different things at the same time. It is one steady vision, through the risen Lord, of this world progressing into its transcendence.

For it is not as though the world-to-come has nothing to do with this world. Whatever world will come in the resurrection that Jesus promises all of us will be the flowering of what he has done in his followers through the Spirit in this world.

Can we expect a better world without putting down the one we have? Can we seek eternal life without disparaging the years that are given? Can we seek to be saints here, amidst our tenements and autos and computers and harvesters, without saying that we are working only to be saints hereafter? Can we let the power of God envelop all of creation, living and dead, past, present and future, in one grand vision of redemption and transformation?

"Yes," says our faith. Because God has said "yes" to us.

Questions

When did time and history begin?

Time and history began with creation. Before creation, time did not exist.

What is creation?

Creation is the act by which God freely makes all things from nothing. By this, Christians understand that God is not forced

---

CREATION

We are familiar with popular debates between the "creationists" and the "evolutionists," as if God could not have used evolution to bring about the creation of life forms! In fact, evolution is not a denial of creation but a modification of the particular creation account given in the Bible's first book, Genesis.

In Genesis, however, we do not have only one creation story. We have two! In the first one, Genesis 1:1–2:4, God's decree makes the world using the image of the Jewish work week: six days of work, one day of sabbath rest. In the second story (which appears to be the older one), beginning with Genesis 2:4, and continuing with the account of the story of the first sin, God creates humans before any other life forms. This story uses the image of the potter who works with clay.

In the development of Jewish thought, the doctrine of creation came from their experience of God's care for them in history and even through history's tragedies. The final chapters of the prophet Isaiah (64–66) weave together themes of creation and salvation: God's care for his people in their suffering and exile from the holy land is like creation itself!

to create and that all creation is the result only of his love. Everything apart from God was created by him.

When did creation stop?

Creation continues and will continue as long as finite being exists.

How do Christians see the future?

Christians think of the future as something open to the power and action of God. Our existence has all the possibilities that God wills for it and that God wants to bring about.

Do Christians believe that God acts in history?

Christians believe that God is always present in the world, guiding all events and all creation.

What do we call this guidance of God?

We call this guidance "providence," which comes from the word roots meaning to "see ahead." In his providence, God's care "foresees" history and time. Whatever events occur, they cannot frustrate God's ultimate and loving purpose.

If God guides all history, are people truly free?

God guides all history and guides people whom he created with true freedom. In fact, no one would be free or could act in freedom without God's creative love. God's providence acts in history while respecting and making use of our freedom.

Does God cause all things?

God creates all things. He does not directly cause all things. God's providence works through the forces of the universe and through human freedom to bring about his divine goals.

What are the goals of God in history?

God desires to bring all people into the fullness of life and the harmony of peace. This involves relating people to him and

GOD'S GUIDANCE

"Have you not understood? Since the earth was founded he sits enthroned above the vault of the earth, and its inhabitants are like grasshoppers; he stretches out the heavens like a veil, spreads them out like a tent to dwell in. He brings princes to nought and makes the rulers of the earth as nothing. Scarcely are they planted or sown, scarcely is their stem rooted in the earth, when he breathes upon them and they wither, and the stormwind carries them away like straw. To whom can you liken me as an equal? says the Holy One." (Isaiah 40:21–24)

"Praised be the God and Father of our Lord Jesus Christ, who has bestowed on us in Christ every spiritual blessing in the heavens. God chose us in him before the world began, to be holy and blameless in his sight, to be full of love. He likewise predestined us through Christ Jesus to be his adopted sons—such was his will and pleasure—that all might praise the glorious favor he has bestowed on us in his beloved. It is in Christ and through his blood that we have been redeemed and our sins forgiven, so immeasurably generous is God's favor to us. God has given us the wisdom to understand fully the mystery, the plan he was pleased to decree in Christ, to be carried out in the fullness of time: namely, to bring all things in the heavens and on earth into one under Christ's headship. (Ephesians 1:3–10)

relating them to each other. This was the heart of the ministry and preaching of Jesus, which began the revelation of God's kingdom in our world. When God's kingdom is fully revealed, history's goals will have been fully achieved.

When will these goals come about?

God is bringing about these goals even now. Only when creation is fulfilled, however, will these goals be completely attained.

How do we know that God has these goals and plans?

We know the goals of God through his actions in revelation: the history of the Jewish people, in which he first formed his

THE END OF THE WORLD

Many people have been preoccupied about the end of the world—even in our own day, there are those who try to predict it.

We have, however, biblical testimony that this question, arising in the earliest New Testament times, was ultimately left to God—that is, that it is God's task to pick the time when creation would come to its fulfillment.

Paul assures the people of Thessalonica that the living will have no advantage over the dead when the Lord comes; his coming will be swift ("at the command of the archangel's voice and God's trumpet") and we shall all be with the Lord "unceasingly." (1 Thessalonians 4:13–18)

Jesus says that the final days lie in his Father's hands; not even the Son knows "the day or the hour." (Mark 13:32) Likewise, Peter consoles his people, who wondered about the Lord's "delay," by quoting the psalms: "One day is as a thousand years and a thousand years are as a day." (2 Peter 3:8, citing Psalm 90:4)

The Bible, then, strives to make us more concerned about the reality of our judgment and the world's fulfillment rather than the time when these things will happen. Whereas we can do nothing about the time, we can certainly respond to the reality of our judgment, whether it be tonight or in a billion years.

people, and the death and resurrection of Jesus, in which human nature came to the fullness of life.

What does the resurrection of Jesus have to do with history?

Jesus fulfills the goals of God in his resurrection because he attains the fullness of life and bestows unity and peace on all those united with him. Jesus is the future of every person. He is the first one to experience the completion of God's kingdom in his human life. In him, all humans can experience history's completion.

When will history be complete?

No one knows the date when history will be completed. We know it will reach fullness when all are raised to life by Christ.

THE FUTURE LIFE

What will the experience of life's fullness be like?

We can only guess what the fullness of life will be like. We know that it will be a share in the risen glory of Jesus in which the limitations of our bodies, minds and spirits will be over-

---

THE FUTURE LIFE

Paul thinks of the future life as fulfillment, passing to the ultimate and direct knowledge of God in which all will be grasped, all will be loved in God. He compares this life with the future life, reasoning:

> *"Our knowledge is imperfect and our prophesying is imperfect. When the perfect comes, the imperfect will pass away. When I was a child, I used to talk like a child, think like a child, reason like a child. When I became a man, I put childish ways aside. Now we see indistinctly, as in a mirror; then we shall see face to face. My knowledge now is imperfect; then I shall know even as I am known."* (1 Corinthians 13:9–12)

In the same letter, he tries to reason about the nature of heaven, particularly the kind of bodies we will have in glory. "Earthly men are like the man of earth, heavenly men are like the man of heaven. Just as we resemble the man from earth, so shall we bear the likeness of the man from heaven," he writes. "The dead will be raised incorruptible and we shall be changed. This corruptible body must be clothed with incorruptibility, this mortal body with immortality." (See 1 Corinthians 15:48–49, 52–53)

John's first letter echoes Paul's sense of personal achievement, showing the connection between our present status with God and our future life with him:

> *"Dearly beloved, we are God's children now; what we shall later be has not yet come to light. We know that when it comes to light, we shall be like him for we shall see him as he is. Everyone who has this hope based on him keeps himself pure, as he is pure."* (1 John 3:2–3)

come because of the harmony we will have with God and others. We will live in perfect love with God and others. We will pass beyond the brokenness, pain and frustration of our present life and we will not experience death again.

Will all people come to this fullness of life?

All those who are in union with God will experience life's fullness.

Will there be any who do not come to this fullness?

Those who are estranged from God and others, living by greed, violence, bitterness and hatred, will not be able to experience the fullness of life.

What do we call this state of fullness?

Christians call this state in which we attain the fullness of life "heaven."

Is anyone living in the state of heaven now?

Catholics believe that all those who die in union with God begin to live this state of fullness even before they are raised bodily.

What do we call those who are living this state of fullness?

Catholics, applying an ancient term from the Bible, call these people "saints."

Who are the greatest saints?

Catholics regard as the greatest of saints Mary, the mother of Jesus, who gave her life in service of her Son, forming the atmosphere of his emotional and physical growth and standing by him in his ministry and death. She is the model of faithful discipleship for all who would follow Jesus. So great a saint is Mary that Catholics believe, according to ancient traditions, that she lives in the fullness of heaven, body and soul. In addition to honoring Mary as Mother of Jesus (and,

THE HAIL MARY

Catholics honor Mary, the Mother of Jesus, with the famous prayer called "The Hail Mary." The prayer has two parts: the first echoes the words of St. Luke's angel who announced to Mary that she would be the Mother of Jesus (see Luke 1:28ff.); the second part asks Mary's help and care in our lives. We can ask Mary to help us, along with all the other saints, because she and they are members of our Christian family. In union with Christ, they show his care and love by their prayer and spiritual influence. In the family of God, all care for each other, whether living or dead. This relationship we call "the communion of saints."

Hail Mary, full of grace,
the Lord is with thee:
blessed art thou among women,
and blessed is the fruit of thy womb, Jesus.
Holy Mary, Mother of God, pray for us sinners,
now and at the hour of our death. Amen.

therefore, Mother of God), Catholics also give great honor to St. Joseph, Mary's husband and Jesus' foster-father, to St. John the Baptist who prepared Jesus' ministry, and the apostles who followed Jesus in his ministry and were empowered by the Holy Spirit after his resurrection.

Are there many kinds of saints?

There are *martyrs*, who have died in witness to Christ; *virgins*, who have lived with hearts focused only on Christ; *pastors*, who have taught and preached the Gospel in their words and their deeds; *missionaries*, who have preached the Gospel to those who never heard it; *married men and women*, whose lives have mirrored God's love and faithfulness; and *single men and women* of outstanding charity who have spent their lives with the poorest and most rejected.

Before history is complete, what happens to people who die?

Those who die either begin to experience the fullness of life as saints, pass through a state of purification prior to this fullness, or live out their choice of being estranged from God and others.

What do we call this state of estrangement?

This state is known as "hell." There have been many images of hell, from Jesus himself to those of great poets. What all these images have in common is the sense of frustration in being estranged from God and others forever.

Why is there a state of purification?

Because so many people live without their whole heart turned toward the message of the Gospel, they still are in need of further conversion before they can begin to experience the fullness of God's life. Catholics call this state "purgatory" to emphasize its transforming character.

How long does this state of purification last?

Time does not mean the same thing for the dead as for the living. As long as we are in need of conversion and have not opened our hearts to the fullness of life in God, we will need to be prepared and purified.

How long does "hell" last?

If one dies separated from God and others, he or she can never become open to the fullness of life that God offers. Therefore, the state of frustration we call "hell" does not end.

Is anyone in hell?

We do not know if anyone is in hell. Certainly, God's love and mercy tries to touch and open the heart of every person; God desires even more than we that we come to the fullness of life. Still, we know from history that people can close themselves off from others and from all human and personal values. In doing this, they cut themselves off from God as well.

Should a person worry about going to hell?

Jesus did not come to make us worry, but to console us with the assurance of God's love and care. He wanted us to worry

JUDGMENT

Through Jesus' discussion with the Sadducees (the group of Jewish leaders who did not believe in the existence of angels or spirits or human souls after death), we know that he clearly taught the existence of the human person beyond physical death. The God of Abraham, Isaac and Jacob, Jesus says, is the God of the living; therefore they are alive. "All are alive in God," he concluded. (Luke 20:27-38)

Just as clearly, Jesus taught God's judgment over us after this life—a judgment that leads either to the joys of the saved or the sorrows of the damned. Sometimes he used a simple parable to teach this:

"The reign of God is like a dragnet thrown into the lake, which collected all sorts of things. When it was full, they hauled it ashore and sat down to put what was worthwhile into containers. What was useless, they threw away. That is how it will be at the end of the world. Angels will go out and separate the wicked from the just and hurl the wicked into the fiery furnace, where they will wail and gnash their teeth." (Matthew 13:47-50)

Jesus' idea of "hell" comes from the valley to the south of Jerusalem called "Gehenna." It was a place of pagan ritual and child sacrifice since ancient times, held abominable since the days of the prophets. Jesus used the idea of his contemporaries to make Gehenna into an image of ultimate failure, isolation and suffering.

He shows, too, that judgment, including heaven and hell, springs from the relationships we have with each other and with him. "The judgment of condemnation," Jesus says, "is this: the light came into the world, but men loved darkness rather than the light because their deeds were wicked." (John 3:19) Jesus certainly conceived of the state of hell as unending and utterly miserable. (cf. Matthew 18:8-9)

No parable gives the personal nature of God's judgment better than the story of the King who comes at the end of time:

"When the Son of Man comes in his glory, escorted by all the angels of heaven, he will sit upon his royal throne, and all the nations will be assembled before him. Then he will separate them into two groups, as a shepherd separates sheep from goats. The sheep he will place on his right hand, the goats on his left. The King will say to those on his right: 'Come. You have my Father's blessing! Inherit the Kingdom prepared for you from the creation of the world. For I was hungry

and you gave me food, I was thirsty and you gave me drink. I was a stranger and you comforted me, in prison and you came to visit me.' Then the just will ask him: 'Lord, when did we see you hungry and feed you or see you thirsty and give you drink? When did we welcome you away from home or clothe you in your nakedness? When did we visit you when you were ill or in prison?' The King will answer them: 'I assure you, as often as you did it for one of my least brothers, you did it for me.' "

Next, the King addresses those on his left, sending them to "that everlasting fire prepared for the devil and his angels." For when he was hungry, thirsty, naked, in prison, a stranger and in need, they did not help.

"Then they in turn will ask: 'Lord, when did we see you hungry or thirsty or away from home or naked or ill or in prison and not attend to you in your needs?' He will answer them: 'I assure you, as often as you neglected to do it to one of these least ones, you neglected to do it to me.' These will go off to eternal punishment and the just to eternal life.'' (Matthew 25:31–35)

more about being faithful to God and serving others than about the future of our soul. If we seek first his kingdom, he says, then everything, including heaven, will be given to us.

HOPE AND OUR WORLD

Do Christians work only for the fullness of life in heaven?

Heaven only comes about through the transformation of the present life. We cannot be concerned about the fullness of life without being concerned about the life that is given to us now. Christians express their hope for a fullness of life through their commitment to this present world.

What kinds of commitments do Christians have in the world?

Christians believe that everyone born has a right to those things necessary for life: food, housing, work, education and faith. Justice demands that we struggle to secure these rights

THE NEW HEAVENS—THE NEW EARTH

The visionary John, whose Book of Revelation has permanently shaped all imagination about the future, comes closest to the dreams of Christians—indeed, of all people—concerning the life to come, the world that God is making.

> "Then I saw new heavens and a new earth. The former heavens and the former earth had passed away, and the sea was no longer. I also saw a new Jerusalem, the holy City, coming down out of heaven from God. . . . I heard a loud voice from the throne cry out: 'This is God's dwelling among men. He shall dwell with them and they shall be his people and he shall be their God who is always with them. He shall wipe every tear from their eyes and there shall be no more death or mourning, crying out or pain, for the former world has passed away.'" (Revelation 21:1–4)

John is only continuing the dreams expressed as long ago as the ancient prophets, such as Isaiah, who talks about God creating "new heavens and a new earth; the things of the past shall not be remembered or come to mind. Instead there shall always be rejoicing and happiness in which I create."

> " Before they call, I will answer; while they are yet speaking, I will hearken to them. The wolf and lamb shall graze alike, and the lion shall eat hay like the ox. None shall hurt or destroy on my holy mountain, says the Lord." (Isaiah 65:17ff.)

not only in theory but in fact. Justice is the basis of human dignity. Only when people have the means to live as humans can they sense dignity and worth in their lives.

Do Christians strive for peace?

Justice, while seeking the basic rights of everyone, also demands peace because war deprives people of the right to live securely.

May a Christian ever fight or go to war?

A Christian may fight, personally and for his nation, only to keep another from doing greater harm to him. In this sense,

Christians have justified a limited and defensive war. However, no Christian is ever obliged to fight in a war judged unjust or immoral; no Christian may violate his or her conscience by being forced to fight.

Do Catholics support nuclear weapons?

Catholics pray for the day when nuclear weapons will be completely eliminated. No weapon that could bring such devastation to people and the world can ever be justified; nothing could ever make the use of these weapons acceptable. Because of this, most Catholics will not tolerate even the threat of the *use* of such weapons. These weapons are a direct assault on the hope that Christians have for fullness of life and the world's transformation.

Is Christian hope justified?

Christian hope for the fullness of life seems like silliness in view of a history that is pocked with violence, greed, war and death. But Christians are not naive and never pretend to live in a world other than the real one. The resurrection of Jesus

---

CONFIDENCE IN GOD

"If God is for us, who can be against us? Is it possible that he who did not spare his own Son but handed him over for the sake of us all will not grant us all things besides? Who shall bring a charge against God's chosen ones? God, who justifies? Who shall condemn them? Christ Jesus who died—or rather, who was raised up and who is at the right hand of God and who intercedes for us? Who will separate us from the love of Christ? Trial, or distress, or persecution, or hunger, or nakedness or danger or the sword? I am certain that neither death nor life, neither angels nor principalities, neither the present nor the future, nor powers, neither height nor depth nor any other creature, will be able to separate us from the love of God that comes to us in Christ Jesus our Lord." (Romans 8:31ff.)

HOPE AND JUSTICE

The entrance of the Church into politics took place as soon as Christianity began; no individual, let alone group, can isolate himself from the world and its movements. Neither can, nor does, the Church.

Since the end of the nineteenth century, the Church has been involved in a very conspicuous way in the dialogue about society—its rights, powers and responsibilities. Cry as some do that the Church should stick to the Gospel, the Gospel itself still forces the Church to come face to face with the world.

Singular documents have come from the Popes and the Second Vatican Council about the modern world and the place of justice in it. For the denial of justice is also the denial of God's order in the world. Popes have written about justice through the use of encyclicals; the most famous have been:

Rerum Novarum, 1891, by Pope Leo XIII, on the conditions of the working class.

Quadragesimo Anno, 1931, by Pope Pius XI, which furthers the arguments of *Rerum Novarum*.

Mater et Magistra, 1961, and *Pacem in Terris*, 1963, by Pope John XXIII, both arguing for a just world order.

Progressio Populorum, 1967, by Pope Paul VI, which continues the thought of John XXIII, but applies it specifically to aspects of the world economic order and the arms race.

Gaudium et Spes, written during the Second Vatican Council, discusses justice and peace issues that range across the whole of the twentieth century.

happened after his shameful, violent and unjustifiable death. In this event, history and life already hit the bottom. Because Jesus passes through human defeat to reveal and bring the fullness of life, Christians can justify their hope in Jesus. No amount of failure, defeat or hatred can frustrate the purposes of God.

Epilogue
The Continuing Search

Thank God for next steps.

Next steps mean that we have some place to go that is appropriate. Some place that makes sense. Some place that will let us pursue our projects and searches as ourselves.

If there were no next steps, either our project would be completed or we would have to guess some giant leap that may well frighten even the best jumpers.

What is your next step? What is being asked of you? Some giant leap into a new religion, a new community, a new way of life? Or a trip to the library to read up on one or two items that provoked thought? Or a trip to a friend's house to have some coffee and toss around one or two ideas?

Whatever your next step is, please be aware that it is yours. You are the only one who can seek, who can ask the questions that you want to ask, who knows what a real answer sounds like. No one's questions will be quite like yours, because no one has had the experience that you have had.

What you need to know is that there is a next step for you. You can find the appropriate response to wherever you find yourself at this point in your spiritual life.

The search for faith is a curious interplay with what is going on inside us and our "family" in the particular and wider sense of that word. For no search happens totally between the ears: it happens in the dynamic relationship between a particular person and other particular persons. If we could know and understand and love everything by ourselves, there would be quite a bit of loneliness in the world. And isolation. And fracturing.

But we never are really alone, even in the deepest and quietest questions of our souls. Because of that, we can count on the support of others.

Big changes may scare us and generate a lot of solid resistance from others—and from ourselves. Old Isaac Newton's *inertia* applies to more than bodies in a vacuum; it applies to so many human beings who find it more comfortable to freeze and flinch than to take the next step.

But the next step need not be big or frightening. It need not be the leap we don't feel ready to make. It can be as appropriate and as tailored as desired.

Even if you, for example, want to join an RCIA program in the local parish, this is not the final step, nor does your name go on the dotted line in indelible ink. The RCIA, in fact, is designed to further "inquiry," to help you search in a supportive community that will aid any steps you may choose to take thereafter.

You picked up this book because faith, God, Jesus and truth are all important to you. You have the kind of heart and soul that seeks what is real and ultimate.

And that is precisely what will show you your next step: your own quest for what is real and ultimate, your own journey to God and his peace.

Respect that quest. Listen to his voice. Struggle with his call. Feel his peace. Face those who are his people. Then your next step will be done with the integrity and truth that, really, will be the only things you'll have to bring to God when your inquiry comes to its final step in heaven.

Questions

What does God ask of me?

God asks of any person that he or she be honest and try to listen to the deepest longings of the self.

What does God ask me to give up?

God, who created us "good" and loves us, wants us to give up nothing of our personal integrity, dignity or dreams. One of the ways we guide our search is by always returning to the values implicit in our human life.

How do I discover God?

Through myself, in my dreams and hopes, as I strive for honesty and dignity, I try to make sense of my world. It is in this quest, in my relationships with others and the world, that I will discover overtures to God.

Is God obvious in my life?

After we discover God, he is obvious. Until then, it may well be a search in the dark in which I *cannot* know the outcome until I arrive at it. We must be honest in all our searching.

What will help me in the search for God?

If I am honest with myself, I will ask questions and seek new experiences. I will also be open to the experiences and teachings of others. The quality of their searches and witness will be an important help in my own search for God.

Is Jesus important in the search for God?

For Christians, Jesus is *decisive* in the search for God. For all people, however, Jesus' experience of God and his relationships with others remain an unparalleled example of what the human journey toward God is like. To what extent does my experience match the experience of Jesus? To what extent does his experience bring me beyond my own?

How do I discover the experiences of Jesus?

We have a way of entering the mind of Jesus through the Scriptures. They contain the witness of those who were most influenced by Jesus; the impact of Jesus on them enters our own lives through our prayerful reflection on these writings. They open me to the values, commitments and dreams that he espoused.

AN ENCOUNTER WITH JESUS

The Samaritan woman only wanted water. Jesus met her, but not as the "enemy" and "stranger" Samaritans were supposed to be. He took her need and showed it was deeper than she thought. When Jesus offered her water, she smartly remarked: "Sir, you don't even have a bucket. How can you get water from the well?" Jesus replied:

"Everyone who drinks this water [from the well] will be thirsty again. But whoever drinks the water I give him will never be thirsty; no, the water I will give him shall become a fountain within him, leaping up to provide eternal life."

The woman naively asks for this water, thinking it means a faucet in her home—she won't have to come to the well anymore!

"Go, call your husband, and then come back here." "I have no husband." "You are right in saying you have no husband! The fact is you have had five, and the man you are living with is not your husband. What you said is true." "Sir, I can see you are a prophet . . ."

A prophet who tells the future? Or a prophet who sees the hurts, the hungers, the thirsts of a heart?

"Sir, I know there is a Messiah coming." "I who speak to you am he."

The next thing she knows, she is running into the town, yelling, "Come and see someone who told me everything I ever did! Could this not be the Messiah?"

The woman from Samaria could only ask this question because she was open to his probing and open to probing him. She could have cut the dialogue off at any point. But she let it go on until she found herself saying: "Could not this, in fact, be the Messiah, the one for whom I've been waiting?" (See John 4:4ff.)

With whom can I discuss my religious questions?

All true believers enjoy talking with one who is really searching. In the Catholic Church, the local parish has many people with whom questions can be honestly discussed. The clergy receive many years of training; counselors and teachers also have backgrounds for exploring issues that seekers raise.

Are there things I need to pay special attention to in my search?

Should anyone try to force answers to questions, especially ones you have not asked, you should beware. Should anyone not prize your own experience and resist your growing from it, you should also beware. Should anyone ask you to deny basic human values and insights which you have discovered, you should beware. Similarly, you should refrain from asking people to solve all your problems for you, from wanting simplistic answers to very deep questions, and from demanding of others a perfection or posture that is frankly unreal.

When can I begin to pray?

To search sincerely is already to begin praying. We need belong to no formal church to open our hearts to God in prayer.

What kinds of questions should I be asking?

The hardest work in the world is coming up with the right questions. Everyone will have different ones, coming from his or her special life experiences. Only *your* questions should be asked; only *your* questions can be answered for you. The brilliance of faith is that it responds to the varying questions of so many people—the same faith touches on so many different lives in such deep ways!

How long will my search take me?

If ours is a true search, no one can—or should—know how long it will take. Searching is a strange activity. One wanders

---

TESTIMONY OF THE BLIND MAN

"He put mud in my eyes. I washed it off and now I can see. . . . He is a prophet. . . . I know this much: I was blind before; now I can see." (John 9:15, 17, 25)

in the woods for years and, all of a sudden, walks into the clearing, unexpectedly. Such an illumination, after so much darkness, is what Christians mean by grace. God's constant gift of grace breaks upon us in its sudden, brilliant realization. All of a sudden, we are changed. All of a sudden, we are home. All of a sudden, we have found that for which we have always searched.

Topical Index

The topical index has two sections; the first one indexes special material presented in box form in the text; the second indexes the important references to topics.

Index of Boxed Material

Scriptural Index

This index also comes in two sections. The first is an index of citations in which you will find the cited Scripture reproduced for reading and meditation. The second is an index of references which indicates on what pages the referred passages can be found.

Index of Scriptural Citations